#Enough

Stop the school killings. Stop the political wars. Stop the towerists, plus stop its presence that will be coming to the future of the country that has a blind side so we can stop this part from falling apart. The wisdom of foresight can be learned and shared.

To the Youth

If you can't stand the truth don't stop reading!

It is time to back this problem up out of sight

The Lord wants the youth's attention. Now that he has it can we see eye to eye with him?

We will be ready for 2025

Written by the Holy Spirit
Co-written by Bro. Tracy Bush

Dedicated to:

To all the youth who have died in a school. Their spirits still reside with us. We are thankful for them. This is also dedicated to all people who are dedicated to stopping Satan's dieconomie. I thank the Lord for this. I hope the teachings will provide safety in everyone's life.

I have a birthday that falls on February 27th, which is also the anniversary of the killing of students at Chardon High School in Ohio. I honor the memory of them all.

Foreword

This may be one of the biggest cross-roads that has one of the most important meanings to it. We as a people must not let this pass us by. To get to the point the devil is the greatest illusion impressionist that makes people think we have something right when we aren't. It causes us to not see the truth and how many are tricked by this? Well, it happens again. The young man got tricked by Satan again. What I mean is he had no rational thinking at his ability to use so he didn't relate to but one thing that has been building up inside of him, ugliness. The hate showed up to show out and that is what happened. Now there is no reason for this misfortune to show itself again with this truth and guidance.

This can be stopped because there are people who need a process of freedom from it. This can be for a watchman to be on the inside of someone who has been somewhat deprived of love and even more someone who is unprotected and needs spiritual food to grow.

Therefore, to put the pieces together about what the problem is that causes the acts of violence at schools it comes from the lack of the right kind of food. It is not the eatable kind, it is the kind that can't be seen by eyesight but will fill the spirit up that will make people well.

We talk about the mental problems people are having and not the spiritual one. It can be needed more than the first one and if it doesn't get fixed, oh well it may be a hit or miss just trying to work on the mental. I can't say that what I say may work for everyone but if you want to help someone don't try one without the other.

The youth that killed the 17 people was lost out of touch with no kind of spiritual food or it may have been given to him in the wrong way. That is right, some of what people teach others is unhealthy to take in. That is why we need to tool up with new news.

I will go as far as to say that we are a nation of people who are on the wrong track in ways that I can only speak about. The Lord wants me to let "them people" know, they need to become "we people."

I say this because the gun that fired the shot that was heard around the world has been the one thing that has grown out of proportion. The status of this possibly has not stopped but created the bigger capacity of weapons for homes and in return it has caused more pain in the homes and streets of America than anything else. What do I really want to say? It is that we have lost our way because of this. That is right, we have been so blinded with a kind of pride to want to have and possess the power to stop someone from living.

It has taken on a presence of its own. It has created darkness in places of love. The fact of the matter is, the weapons have replaced God in some people's homes. It has done this to a certain degree that a large part of our nation believes if they do not have a weapon when and if a homeland war of any kind breaks out, they won't be able to kill someone legally. This doesn't have anything to do with protecting themselves. How sick is this? Is this the satanic sickness that blinds people and freezes the love of God? All I can say is maybe so, but we reap what we sow. Killings by youth are a part of the unseen madness that lies under the rock that hides the snake, Satan.

If we were our brothers' keepers then there could be an honest effort to stop the harm of the youth in the schools in our land but to take a look at it as if it is a tip of an iceberg that has not run its course, is the only way to help stop it now. All the noise and yelling won't do any good because this has only been testing ground for the big mayday that will come if we do not let the "you people" know to become the "we people." I say this because the change is needed to disarm us of weapons such as guns and arm ourselves with the blessings of spiritual food and guidance. This will protect us more than any weapon as or in the body of Christ.

The fear that people have been developing of a war on a man to man basis is wrong. It will not be like that. It will be a spiritual war that will take place and not Armageddon. It will be a test of mankind's faith in the Lord to believe he has got this and if we fail when the real deal comes there will be many more lives lost to hell.

The next seven years we are to be prepared not to take up arms but the Bible to use as our shield against the prince of darkness. Open your eyes this is the time to get prepared. Let's be about our father's business. I say that because Satan has been testing the fire to see how hot he can get it for his people who are lost out of the hands of God.

The shootings are his test-grounds that is right, he is real. However, being the master of illusion is what he is best at. The Lord is unveiling him to his believers, to stop this problem and get the word out to feed the people spiritual food in schools. It cannot hurt, but do not force it on anyone.

Youth: you are the future of the USA: look over your home and think for the adults in them somewhat to see if they need help getting out of the earthly warring spirit and show them it is not just that your mind needs to be renewed but your spirit because it is just Satan trying to throw you off to not be able to see what is really happening. The fact that the hands-on approach to war is the quickest way to go that you people know because you lack the spiritual skills. So "you people" become "we people" to stand for what is right together.

Please do not let that one shot blow the one shot to keep the country's blessings flowing so we all can receive some of them.

Which one? Parable or paraphrasing. Do I know? Do we sometimes use what man made for bad? We as agents of the Lord use for good will. I think so and hope you do too.

 Note to not be affected by any adverse parts of 2025

I will say I cannot say how this seven years in waiting will unfold but what I will say is we must not get into any kind of a greater spiritual war between each other that creates more separation in the USA than we are now. I have looked at one of the main components of starting any kind of war. It is a political war that starts in the government of any country. This kicks off a kind of people war that grows into a spiritual war.

No man should try to fight a spiritual war alone, because only the Lord can win unless you get a special blessing and anointing to do this. So far I have known of only one in the history of the world who was called to do that, Jesus was one! Know that the Holy Spirit, the Comforter is there to handle that along with God's angels who are prepared to deal with spiritual wars.

It is time to stop letting Satan keep catching us off guard. It is time to freeze frame the work that Satan has been doing hurting the young and old. The teachers do not deserve the pain for the youths losing their lives.

What may help the teachers is the fact that students will be more pleased with themselves after they are exposed to the new learning tools that come in this book. They may not be in a good position from neglect. Some of the systems they had to teach along with a not so great pay level in some geographical locations.

This information will also help give a parent/guardian a breath of fresh air while adding relief to help with their peace of mind as their children attend school.

Warning

This reading is recommended for ages 16 and up. If there is any problem with anyone who is confused about what they have read tell to someone about it. I also recommend some parents read this book with their child. I do recommend if people can make time to start reading groups to go over this book and others I recommend and I wish all a great learning experience.

This can be the best part of God's laws that you get the one on one with that he affords to everyone. This will create the renewal of the spirit and bring forth a kind of secret wisdom out of you that I can't speak on. It will be for you to know and show when the Lord says it is time to work. My life has turned into a kind of pilgrimage. That is what it seems like to show the love the Lord afforded me, even though I wasn't worth. It lets people know if he can do it for me surely he will do it for you. The fact remains I can't tell everything he did.

The things we do in the laws of the Lord for most is, let him clean the heart from sin and refrain also the heart from committing sin.

Our spiritual father will help us abort our sin nature will. It is a hard and because of the distraction of the world. It is needed to have some extra time to spend in the will of the father where you can still lose yourself in from the rest of the hustle and bustle of the world to a place of inner peace as if you are in some place in the world far from the modern so-called civilization. This can be the kind of dream you can ask the Lord for to refresh your life daily.

A Message for You

This can be a place to find inner peace. Take it home
to share it with the adults or guardians in your life.
This is an introduction to a library of wealth that
money can only pay for the paper but not the words
on it or the image of wisdom to be received that is
priceless. It is to be known as a positive force of
energy that is being released daily in the atmosphere
that is reaching up into the hemisphere of mankind's
spiritual growth.

Be a part of the wisdom to share the manifestation of
life to be had or lost from. Are you or do you know
what entitlements package consists of? If there is a
pie-chart of love, how much of the pie do you know of
that belongs to you or are you settling for whatever
comes your way even if you are getting
shortchanged? Check the chart of inventory within
this information with the less you have to receive
more of what you need. Read to know if you have
been approved for more than you have. If you do not
know, you will not get it. Do not sleep your blessings
away so you will obtain them.

This is a vehicle to help balance the scales that create
more justice for helping people out of poverty on
many levels of life. Inquiring minds should want to
know what it takes and how it can be done. The big
problem we have is the lack of wisdom.

This is a poem I wrote many years ago: whether the weather be hot, whether the weather be cold, weather the weather whatever the weather whether you like it or not. It has helped many to see how to live within a different state of growth. I hope it can comfort you at a time of need.

Do you prepare your child or young adults to be able to weather these kinds of storms the best you can? Well, there is a well of knowledge that you can add to what you have already to not send them out in the world unclothed. Being clothed properly adds an additional covering as an umbrella over them to present them with more of the love you may not be able to supply them. Knowing it and showing is not the same.

This is the level of letting the Lord supply you with spiritual skills you can learn from this. It can be considered a home learning program and therapy treatment prevention school in a book to help stop a level of crookedness that is out in the world.

To sit down with them and take the books I have been blessed to learn from and share with my children and now my grandchildren. It is a light of heavenly blessings I hope that you come to know and share with a child you know. They may need the new added protection in their life.

This is for anyone who thinks they may have missed a beat in their child's life. This is a part of the ugly face that a multitude of people need help with. So many put on a fake smile to cover up the pain that can be stopped to enhance the opportunity to create positive energy to flow throughout the nation, as well as help put out firestorms that are created by individuals with dust devil attitudes about life and want to stop liberty and the pursuit of happiness.

In conclusion to this example, we will identify this process as a plan of success.

When you help yourself it also gives you a way to put your tithes and offerings into kingdom building work.

This is another chapter of the Bound to Heaven Publishing/Ministries in conjunction with the ecumenical house of God without walls.

Time to Listen

If there are bad influences in your life and you are or may be one also, there is help to guide you in the right direction. Teach yourself to stay out of your own way so you can stay out of trouble. Learn to detour from the hot spots in life that put you in the void-noid numb-dumb sin-drome that is there to trap you into one of Satan's zones. Keep your freedom and advance your life to be able to enjoy a good life as should be. The blessings can be learned in your life then you can learn to live and be happy.

The story of a missing piece
that can be fulfilled to add spiritual skills to your life

As our children, we should show love to them daily and then send them out into the world. We must prepare them to learn and grow up to be smart, strong and safe.

It is our hopes and wishes as adults that we supply them with enough love to sustain them until they have a sustainable supply of their own. Most adults who are responsible for their children around them still may be lacking in what they are in need of and that is the love of the understanding that comes from the Lord. Therefore, they are shortchanged and unfortunately they lack on what they can supply to their child.

This is not a manual to criticize a parent or guardian. It is a presence of a way to understand the pluses that come with a transformation of information that may help to fulfill a space that is in need of wisdom in a young person's life.

To clarify and not to write in to a parable, but to come out of one; A child that is sent out in the world is like the emperor without clothes. If the right spiritual food is not being fed to them daily. Therefore, it is only by the grace of God that they may survive.

To truly try to write the unfolding of a conquest of a dimension of improper growth doesn't require the level of prediction. It is evidenced in the book *Fixing What's Broken in America by Stopping Towerism*, where things were predicted that proved to be true. It gives witness to the spiritual presence of knowledge I was given to share about the towerists of the government. One party has been tossed a curve in a presence of spirit that reveals a chance needed lets this become an easy transition for them.

Forward Thinking

The books deal with the prevention plan that gets to the youth before they run away from themselves and everyone else to help them with ways to work through problems and it is developed with the help of their parent/guardian. Would you like to help?

It took me sixty years to reach this part of life that I didn't want to reveal, this part of life caused much pain and disruption. I never wanted to confront it but I came to a place where there was no other choice. Between ages of 5 and 6 I was violated sexually by an adult that loved me and I loved them but the experience created a wall between me and the person that didn't continue to grow.

I tried to ignore it and act as if it never happened. I used my imagination to shield me because the experience continued to build pain and anguish that grew and caused division in self that eventually led to trying different avenues of detoxifying or thinking what I did, positive or negative, created a cleansing factor when in fact it didn't.

It didn't because I had to endure challenges of making myself aware of facts. These experiences led to deeper level of darkness but only if I allowed myself to go in the direction to a certain measure and there was no control over the emotional roller coaster due to the fact that I was confused about what love was and meant. I heard the word and believed. Still I couldn't display totally or wrap my arms around what it meant as a child to puberty then toward adulthood. It left me a little lost outside of myself but I thank God that I didn't go completely over the edge about it.

It seems I was lost on an odyssey of trial and error as others go through abuse and have to face. At the same time, there were more challenges that I had to face because I was in a dysfunctional family setting, even though it was a full family setting but dysfunctional because of abuse in home between mother and father that guided to another level of misunderstanding about facts of love. The bottom line is they stayed together but I thought they loved because they were together. It was made up due to devastating components then you have learned to develop love without the same criteria regarding those things that were wrong.

In between time there were good times. Not so good times continued as I grew into manhood. I came to recognize but was a force of human error that caused me to judge or view self wrongly. At the same time, taken place outside forces people, places, things developed in me that led me astray to another land of wonder that caused me to find myself in trouble zones due to trouble regarding outside relations.

This became a jungle of dealing with differences between right and wrong that led to me being tarnished dealing with trauma that was faced as a child, along with facts regarding what happened in sequence from child to puberty. This created another incident of being violated and abused between 9 and 10 by female relative.

These courses of disturbing my reality were there to cause a level of self-destruction in such a way that caused personal turmoil. In addition, caused me to go astray labeled as a troubled man at early stage of life. Before aware, I was incarcerated doing time for petty crimes. No one would say, this was a badge of honor (jail/prison). It turned out to be after wearing a badge of stupidity, ignorance and foolishness. The crazy part is I was locked into a system being mentally deranged and morally incompetent but same time was spiritually endowed.

To give you an idea of coming from a presence of worship, God, church and fellowship in my life as far as I remember, about age 2 at least, I say that because recall system in mind gives me opportunity to regulate as it unfolds. Now another horizon of realizing that me being traumatized as a child and abused as a child put me in a frame of darkness. Thanks to the will of Holy Spirit that keeps itself present in my life when unaware it took me through to weather every storm that came my way.

Even when all shadows of darkness fell upon me, my fault or others, assisted me by coasting me, leading me or being caught up on process of the void-noid numb-dumb lame-duck sin-drome was able to maintain a level of guidance that spirit endowed with to come out of madness even though it had big reflection afterward of sadness created from it.

To put things in perspective, at one time I had to stand up against my own father, me and brothers, you cannot be ugly toward my mother anymore. Otherwise, kill me or I'll kill you. Now this happened in early teens. To shed light on facts of being locked up, I still followed faith regardless of how I felt there were services available and I was there. I recommitted myself while in Columbus, Ohio. Now to bring misguided circle there is a need to express.

Whenever a person was locked up in the 70's and shipped out from diagnose center go through as juvenile best place for rehabilitation. I was placed in a place where there was a series of numbers before numbers, letters attached. Letters meant analyzing of circumstances and problems the institution and ideas of what basis they were to create a plan rehab. Out of everyone I knew when I found about system I didn't run from institution with double letters. This meant I was more or less dangerous to others and self emotionally, emotionally unbalanced and prone to violence.

Once I found this out I was taken because I did I really project this to others before found out. As I thought to a certain degree I did. Did things to harm self, used substances to get high levels of danger, all while not being aware of facts that disconnection to reality was taken due to previous abuse. Bridges to life expectations of life were burnt where I couldn't go back across. Was this something that created part of madness, sadness to certain degree to death wish in me regarding life? It pains me to say this existence that drove me to not fear early grave or anything along presence of thought.

I would even take to dimension of feeling something taken away from me something taken away morally striped from me that was tangible. When I was a child I crossed the bridge with my father once. Afterwards, I started crossing by myself and almost lost a friend who I allowed to come with me. This bridge was named the swinging bridge by us who came up behind it. It still stands on Sidaway Avenue on one side and Sidaway Frances on the other one the Kinsman side where I lived.

There was a store on the corner but on the other side was a potato chip factory. Everything was somewhat good until race riots came into play in the mid 1960's and closed bridge to stop fighting between blacks and whites. Connection for free chips because it was too dangerous to go cross again. At the stage of childhood my bridge to growth at a loving existence continued to be ruined by others, other places and things. To learn more about it read the book _What's Going On?_

To see my way clear out of darkness I came to realize as a child I was stealing from the Lord which caused lots of pain and suffering and caused me to begin losing my life. Now as I have mentioned first there is a purpose for my life. That was told to me as a child as I walked through backwoods of Alabama and Mississippi. Now I am thankful for the presence of a state of mind that has guided me to levels of understanding of what love is truly about.

It has been a journey that I would have loved to cut the strings that were attached way before now, that kept me tied into a level of misunderstanding negative emotions and a disruptive conscience and I don't think I need to say more. See, understand and feel the power that we as people created by God have to offer and share among self as one nation not as a separate creation, even though we may come from many different tribes we are all alive because of one reason, the Lord loves us.

Now in order to rebuild the bridge that have been put in place that can't be crossed I feel that if you can see through a vision in your heart through words written you will be connected through a new bridge to bless all mankind, from whatever nation you may reside in as temporary experiences while on earth. I say Amen and Hallelujah.

The key is to put the boneless raw energy at peace

The big part of treatment that comes with the spiritual application of God's order to be put in place of plan that lays out the treatment of love because the seeds are destroyed by the element of the body and its foundation it lives in.

This is therapy for a society for treatment options for potential psychopaths. I have been there and done that. I had trauma but there are kids who don't have trauma and have the problem.

How do we reply to that because it is calling out to the world that it doesn't want to be a part of it because it knows the level of ungodliness it is facing that destroys the conscious state that crosses wires itself that lacks fire with a kind of hell fury that adds up to harm because it foresees the pain it must face. So it is a disruptive state of energy that only the super grace of the love of the Lord can work with because the other half is the gift feel it will be lost in the madness that ensues as growth take place in life.

This is the blind side of an unknown reality that exists in the born gifted born cure that Satan has it out for to kill or steal whatever it can or destroy the gift. Now the opposite is the idiot savant.

What can be done is to dig down with spiritual skills and find that gift and bring to fruition so the dark side can dissipate daily to grow the peace of mind that keeps some safe because they are their biggest downfall and can't be trusted by others.

The broken placenta of the umbilical cord I have called a process of does the problem of a troubled child come to the world because of the mother experience and it may be because by the their not there affect that take place before the child is ever born. It may sound kind of crazy but if we look at SIDS, that kills babies could the disconnection change before the baby is born have a traumatic and harmful change that has long-term effects on a child.

Now if it does it is not a sickness but a spiritual problem that the use of the Lord's tools can fix. If you don't at least try the spiritual skills shop in the book it may be a big mistake to create nothing missing nothing broken. As crazy as it sounds it worked for me and I still live with the trauma in my life.

There are some more research I would like to do but I have no time to do a kind of follow up but I do work with others and do see positive results. Stick the person who has because it is a curse by one means and that is not knowing a cure to help wake up the sincerity of love that are part of the problem from being disconnected place the feet in cold ice water for 5-10 minutes.

Then talk your way out of it and discover the fact that this is done to unfreeze the state of the spiritual disconnection that is making it mentally challenging so we don't fight fire with fire but freeze the fire to feel the love that puts things back into an order that gives a completeness that the outer spirit of negativity has created and the madness that comes along with it that can be removed from someone's life at least to the degree that they are free to not harm themselves and others.

Now how many others have been split down the middle? Could it be a reason that people are now more so attracted to the same sex in some ways?

To round it out or off to let it out it is a force of nature that backfired and to cool it off it takes the Lord's placement of wisdom to protect one's self and to cool it off make a point of knowing you are fixed and to add the cool breeze takes the therapy in 2,4,6,8 times a day and keep it up until it is no longer or keep it for a lifetime if you like it won't hurt another and could help every part of your life.

What is the best treatment? It is to keep it simple.

Let me know that you were hit by a double or maybe triple whammy. I got a breakthrough as anyone can if they believe that you have the power to become supreme over the dark side of nature. Walk in the light that will keep your life right not perfect but right without having to fight because what is happening is unknowingly you are fighting with principalities of darkness that we don't have a way to do unless we are moving in the spiritual realm and the more you are there the less power the enemy has over you also the more the Lord takes the fight away from you.

It's all God's therapy

The less you know about this part of therapy the more Satan will challenge you. If you are not in a spirit felt home it is somewhat worse on a child. It is also the invisible enemy that has a grip on the life of a youth that wants to not let their gift appear to the world.

Does the fear factor come into the division of being lost as the future separation is in place to happen?

Well it could be so this can also be defeated along with the unknown death presence that haunts people that has to take place. We can weigh in on all the levels of misunderstanding to have a complete understanding to know once we have learned the facts of what it does and how it may have come about, the issue of reconnecting the brain breakdown with the spiritual connection of the subconscious. That plays out with madness and sadness because of the ex-placebo umbilical cord breakdown.

This means Satan eats dirt or craps every time you cross my mind. Now you can't touch me any more with the sickness. As for the medicine of pills or that kind of treatment it zombitizes people. I see them on the street and I think this would have been a better treatment.

To keep it real at the time of my growth if I would have known then what I know now, it may not have done me good because I wouldn't have been able to relate the understanding to others. It is hard to believe yourself at a certain time in life. That is why I say now if you don't know what you are learning. Now give yourself some time to work through it so you will know what you know.

I think I wouldn't have survived if I didn't have help from the people that give me the time of day because I fell into a cesspool of death and destruction. I had become a runaway child from myself and I couldn't get away.

The principles of human waste came in to take out my life but thanks to the raising that my parents gave me I had the Lord with me and if not for that I would have perished.

This is part of God's awareness therapy to know the problem that made the troubles that manifested issues can be avoided with God spiritual intervention that is self-taught with a presentation the start with why you don't love self. The reason is that caused it and the solution to stop it from troubling your life.

Regaining Control

A lot of people can't afford the financial placement. This is one reason I have developed this in-house at home help mate to add even greater possibilities to moving forward in the self-healing process that some would rather go at it alone. I recommend an outside source to at least consult with about the problem that has been addressed or undressed to redress it properly, whether it is an addiction that has attached to it or the many other ailments that take a person to a place that causes them to lose something that has something to do with control. This is what you can use to take the fear out of the sting of change.

The top and bottom of it is that phase that has to be regained that gives the rights back to one's life by them having control. This is the achievement that is outlined in the presence of the spiritual skills and gives the Lord the right to control you if anyone or thing must do so.

This process leads to not being or never having to challenge yourself to go down a negative pathway of growth. It puts a limitation of the need to be discontent. The spirit quest has a way of lifting people out of the state of discontentment to keep them in a content state of being and not a disoriented state where there is no peace that comes from having the truth that keeps people free.

I can now say it took me between 45-55 years to totally get out of my woo-woo blues that made me feel somewhat bad about who I was, even though the Lord was with me all the time.

Why do I write this kind of book? During my school-age years I almost killed someone who was a bad person but didn't deserve to be harmed. I was caught up in the madness that made me want to create sadness. Thank God I didn't because I would have been the only fool to hurt someone at a root that was taking place at a high school named Rawlings Junior High during fourth period in Cleveland, Ohio. This is a part of the Cleveland, Ohio silence the guns program.

To understand this plainly, I was innocent at one time and I got damaged and harmed. As I grew, the roots that were set in place developed as I felt, and I subconsciously, I wanted revenge, you could say to a point it made me somewhat crazy. As I grew I didn't want to hurt others so I hurt myself.

Can I be somewhat an exception to the rule and of course there are others like myself that would not harm a child but at the same time there are some that do harm children. This is a part of the void-noid numb-dumb lame-duck sin-drome. But the two-way street is the disconnection from the unity of the mother after the birth that may have untold stories behind it also.

The system is broken. Everyone is paying the price that Satan wants them to pay. The children should never fall through the cracks because a parent did it so wrong that God took them home.

There were 20,000 reported cases of child abuse in Cuyahoga County in 2017. We can increase the help they are in need of that will work toward breaking the cycle and stopping the madness. While we are doing that we can be saving babies from harm because of the failure of one parent also now you want to throw away the key. When this happens everyone loses including the taxpayer. The book *Time to Stop the Abuse* can help with this problem.

Riding with or in a police vehicle

I got used to riding in a police vehicle. I would leave home beginning at about age 3. The police would bring me home numerous times a week. I would wander off and my parents would not be aware of my whereabouts. Perhaps, that is another reason I was locked up as a juvenile in four different institutions and have as an adult been locked up in three different institutions though I visited over eleven jails totally.

Does this mean I would develop a relationship with them? I can only say one the police detectives who locked me up that caught me in committing a crime came to the institution where I was locked up after I was there and he and his wife took me out off grounds to the Brown Derby for a steak dinner.

The fact is I came full circle on not doing the wrong once I was released it helped. But there were more twists and turns before I got somewhat clear of the other side of the law. I stopped looking at them as an enemy.

There is one fact that I would like to add to the picture and that is I had a wondering soul that kept me on the move. I felt left behind also, which didn't help because I thought I had a right to go wherever my father went. I noticed he left me behind but I saw him out and about. It started me on a quest of my own at an early age of about 3. I left home and wandered around the neighborhood to a point that at least 2 or 3 times a week and the police had to help find me.

I look back on this and it gives me insight of the starting of my own. The fury of disappointment has taken place now it is time to put the hope to work.

Hope can stand for – **H**elping **O**ptimistic **P**eople **E**ndure

To All

To some this can be just reassurance that you are, and have been, on the right pathway. For others this can be like an angel touched them for the very first time in the presence of their being. I must say that is not true because you have been touched by an angel before.

You all should know that there are more than enough angels that are waiting for you to let them into your life. All you have to do is open up your heart. Nothing can stop them from sharing their love that gives you the power to succeed in life and the faith you apply to keep building up with love.

I am not trying to overload the system about myself but there were quite a few others traumas that took place in my life and it would take all the pages in this book to explain them. So I will let you know that I have documented lots more about my life in the other books I have authored.

Radical Inclusion

Can this be a part of somewhat ungodly Ouija board that the tricks of Satan display to send people into a down sin-drome that causes them to crash in ways that came about from the void-noid, numb-dumb, lame-duck, sin-drome?

What is the cause of people getting lost in dimensions such as these? The lack of love. Self-love is to know these things that give people a covering to respect themselves and not let the negative ruler take control of their well-being. Living in the presence of your gift is Satan's most important thing to steal from the people who make up the human race. To keep the freedom to not let any title or label take you or keep you in an ungodly bondage is our duty to self and the Lord.

The fact is, a school can bring out the best in you and also the worse of you for you to have to deal with. You don't get any kind of warning and I guess no one else does also.

It is a place that a person who has been wounded can have solitude or a place for a wound to fester. It can be a place that is harmful. If it feels like pain, then the person who is in pain may want to do harm to others.

It can be a place of harm and it can feel painful. This can cause the person in pain to create harm to others.

I got caught up in the madness at a school walk out. I wanted to do harm to someone. It was an unnatural response and I didn't plan it. It came about as a spur of the moment thing and I was stopped by a friend.

The process of fighting that I had was an ongoing problem. I wasn't afraid to use a weapon if I felt I needed, or wanted, to. It was an outlet and I felt I had to cause myself a problem. I went back to jail just to see if I could get a chance to turn pro and maybe make the boxing level that could take me to the Olympics. Having to go back because of my being somewhat locked into the system, I wanted a chance to become a golden glove fighter to win a kind of freedom in Columbus called Herbert Christian.

I did not follow the probation rules and I was returned to do more time. It was a dream I was following to get a break at the golden glove championship and maybe have a long shot at the goal. All I needed to do was train. I lost the main fight to get me on the road. I was transferred to another institution to do more time before I was released.

There was a time when things was backward because I had lots of issues to work through. But as I said I put lots of the trials and tribulations in other books I have authored.

Therapy

What are the problems with youth who act out violence? They get caught up in the crossfire of their developmental principles that trapped them in a confused state of being. They can't get out of it so they think they will have to fight. The violent ways come with the trouble.

Now what is happening? They are being recruited by Satan because of the void-noid, numb-dumb, lame-duck, sin-drome. Their sins outgrow their abilities to think rationally and deadened the conscious to not put reasoning in the front of actions along with consequences.

In others it dead ends the fact that love existed anymore. That is the biggest blinding affect that Satan has in his tool box to take people to hell with him. Stop it with the cool breeze of wisdom that uses joy in your heart.

Take the cool ice feet therapy to heart and do it. It works. Try it even if you don't like it. This is a way to honor the energy that has been put out to be used to turn around any of the negative energy that is left out their hanging. To stop the madness also prevent the sadness that can be stopped.

Youth: end the dumbness of a kid because it is not the gun, it is the madness that wants company. The company is to not share a good time but a bad time like they are going through. To renew this process it takes love of self that can be made new again and again.

This is the second most important tool Satan has to keep this out of mind and out of sight. This gives him a way to get over on people. Stop thinking like this stop him.

Staying in Place not causing Storms

There are plenty of good reading tools out there but the ones to be read are the ones that can extend an intercessory format. These reading tools can give you an outline or projection to help you make the right plan to address road block and stop negativity.

Backing up the wrong force of nature to know what is right will require you to be properly operating in the right environment and not letting the power of inclusion or exclusion hold or fold you.

This requires trust in the conclusion that you are learning for the spirit man inside of you plus acknowledging it is real. Listening to the instincts that are made from love fellowship along with having like-minded people around you and participating for a purpose along with developing a control over staying away from decisions that can paralyze you from being connected to what may help the attitudes of people.

I think about the fact of was it a problem to myself because of what I was experiencing at home at school and in the street life I was a part of also. Was the fact of my learning disability a reason for being locked up in part because of truancy from school?

Once I got back out again I started a new life that got me transferred from one school to another. The school I was to attend was the school of hard knocks. Little did I know it but with the love of the Lord as an inner force in me I had to face the changing of three schools at the same time trying to make a dollar out of fifteen cents, not getting in the way of the law.

I had one tool that got me by even though I lost a best friend in a car crash I was in also along with the fact we were coming from the hospital where another friend of mind was in that died two weeks later. I was saved by lying on a job application saying I was 18 and got a job as a molder in a small foundry. This was to help me get my feet on some kind of solid ground.

That didn't solve the problem I still carry around, such as seeing a guy get killed as a young person having a buddy hang himself as a youth. Besides my drinking problem and the drug use starting off at glue sniffing and drinking along with the drugs that came into play.

But enough of my past because even though my report cards were somewhat bad, I kept a good grade in math but for sure writing. Little did I know at the time it would be a part of my saving grace.

Flatterism

Flatterism is stepping out of darkness into a new light and way of life. Now we turn it up to a state of reputation to build a system in the USA. That got the lead from the British rulers that came about from the towerism. It has run its course.

As the new millennia has shape shifting the way to lead the country into a great place for the people to be and not just the rich and powerful we see a process that has run its course, starting a new chapter of growth that the people need.

It is no longer the norm to be affiliated with so the new consequences are made up of something that must stand out boldly to be known as not like the invisible state of towerism but the dismantling state of flattery that creates the new freedom for all mankind and stops the crippling that came about from depriving people of the love they need. It is as simple as that.

To keep someone in poverty in any way is depriving them and the foremost to give and share is spiritually not realizing that added rules to the state of its well-being to keep an order that makes it a part of a kind of man-made government that is not free because it too adds limitations of a personal issue for some and if we all are one body and true it has branch then why are so many pieces of fruit being soured and dead?

Do you want a cause to help make things right? This may be just what the doctor ordered

If the laws of the government are to protect us from sinning those are the rules of law then it is of a somewhat corrupt state that needs changing.

As I do in some books I wrote if you would like to be a part of making this government new and create change read these books to see a canvas that has already been touched by a brush with paint.

Calm During the Storm
Fixing What is Broken in America by Stopping Towerism
The Power of Knowing "No", (Nos. I and II)
Ending Political Wars in America
The Silver Lining of the 45th President

Also read J.H. Buckley "The Republic of Virtue"

This will help you create the new portrait to be painted. I started it, now who else will join in to help create this beautiful work of art?

It is some of the greatest ways to help stop the corruption in our nation to know about the somewhat wrong ways we have when we can help to make the new pathways we need to go.

Flatterist, flatter him, flattery is, flatters

Flatter yields curves a headwind for risk assets variant perception

It is like a gravitational collapse from massive stars to planets Ensenada

This is the dataism of the times.

Don't flatter yourself anymore because towerism is not cute. You should be praying that cupid comes along and shoots you down out of your tower instead of Satan. He now knows a part of him is revealed and he wants to get to you before the Lord does. The bigger they are the harder they fall, still cupid can put enough arrows in a tower so someone can climb down out of it. The jack up ladder affect is the Lord's way of forgiving the towerists.

The flatterer was created to stop the towerist. Now to help change the course of humanity pray for change to bring about love even when darkness wants to set in. It is always a time for a breakthrough after a state of calamity as the youth in school have been dealing with and this is what is being offered.

It may not be exactly what the doctor ordered, but it still gives better hope for the future for a way to help stop the harm at schools. It also helps show a way to move the tower out of the way that can stop the process the country needs to make in the future.

Well, if that is not shining light on darkness I am speechless, but I think not and you don't have to think not any time soon.

The question I have is, how do you handle getting blindsided by your own sense of direction even though you know you are headed in the right direction? The gravitation of someone, or thing, in life can sideline you and cause you to stop so beware of love in a way that may not be true.

By backing up of the forces of nature that are not properly aligned. The Lord gives you the power to do this.

The real get down

There is a natural draw to the negative level of the void-noid, numb-dumb, lame-duck, sin-drome placement of life, when someone is unprotected in a level of subconscious because of being harmed, hurt, sad, mad or dissatisfied about what is happening in or to their life. It may sound off the beaten path, but I think if we are made out of the earthly foundation of the building parts, aren't we drawn to the right and wrong substances it is made of also? So we can get pulled to the good and not good. That is why we need the pull of the Lord because we are made of him foremost. It is the only part of us that can last forever.

When someone is going through this or through the pathway that can lead down into a darker level of trials and tribulations before you slip into darkness. Withdraw, that is right you have the power and are aware and knowledgeable with wisdom to withdraw yourself ahead of time before the madness takes place and gets control and a hold on you.

It could be temptation to do the things you should not do like having sex, taking drugs, stealing, breaking the law, disrespecting parents and the list goes on. No one is perfect but no one has to be a fool and let the negative activity come out and cause damage to others.

There are many storms always on the horizons as the days go by. That is why the weather changes as does the land. Now to take it a step further, if your child is not properly clothed, they can get sick but if they are it is all good. Now let's look deeper. If the atmosphere in their presence is great outside as far as the eye can see, it may be bringing a different kind of storm on an unseen level where Satan causes harm and even hell.

Not trying to advertise but this is needed

Teens and parents: _The New Added Protection for the Development of Teens and Young Adults at_ Risk. This book will be good for both of you. It may show you something you missed in the welfare of your offspring. This book is 8.5 by 11 and over 200 pages. To add to it you may want to also get a copy of _Time to Stop Living on the Edge_. Believe it or not lots of young people are living there because of not just peer pressure but because of the state of the worldly affairs. It is looming over them like a dark cloud that wants to land on them. It is or may be stifling their ability to feel good about life. This could affect them not knowing about the future and that creates all kinds of uncertainty: the way things may be going at home; the way they are interacting at school.

The other books that I am suggesting to you to read are _A Kaleidoscope of Knowledge_, _Little Mr. Fix-A-Thought_, _A Calling to Become a Watchman_. These are the books in conjunction to the other two already mentioned. This also would be a great way to start your library. The synopsis of these books are on the website.

Why do I write it is not just because I feel it is my gift? It is not because I have made a living off of it. I haven't yet after over 40 yrs. of writing It may be foremost because you matter to me, that if I can tell you anything to advance your life it matters to me, that I do it. Then I hope that someone else's way of life matters to you when you do something for them just because it matters. It matters that we show each other the best way we can to show love. I believe in my heart with my faith that after you read what I write you know you matter to me, Bro Tracy Bush.

One of the reasons I write is as I grew up, I saw some of the people around me who were hurting, because of something that happened in their life and they seemed trapped! I name these places void-noid, numb-dumb, lame-duck, sin-drome. They are the pathways that lead people to Satan stepping into some to do harm.

I mean the adults and they were bitter and it too became a part of their child's life! This painful thing that causes people to not let go or forgive harms them! If they knew the love of God it would have been better for them. I write to help people stay calm during the storms in their life to help save a part of the world from pain and feeling bad!

The worst part about it is I've seen a few of my friends lose their life over the misguidedness of not knowing a greater present of love in their life. Also, for me writing is God's therapy to me! It can be used to help make things better for all people, go to www.boundtoheaven.org.

For the adults you may find something you like there also. Now this can be a good thing for a young lady or man to help increase the life-long learning process that we call spiritual skills.

We look at what it cost for clothing, shoes, coats, etc. If you have to get it off and then some to protect a chance of a child not getting sick, they have to have vaccination shots or medicine to head-off illnesses. That's how it should be so we can look at this as preventive care, just in case. It actually is a kind of Insurance that is being offered at BTHPM. That is of a spiritual element that wants to prevent something negative from sneaking up on you. That is why this kind of ounce of prevention is here. Which add a comfort to life.

This May Not Be You

I write for people's who do not want to believe that they believe there is a God. All they want is any kind of excuse to not go to fellowship or to service to do the will of God, it seems like!

Even with their children because they have some kind of fear, or even think it will make them look weak! So I wrote a book called, _A Message from the Word_. It kind of holds someone's hand and walks them up into the Bible with Love!

To look over the fact that what can influence a person to go into a negative state can be blocked out with the help of these message that had been put in place that create charity to be thankful for. To know you are not damned if you walk through it or leave it open.

The Wrong Process of Thinking

This process could be like having a bad furnace and not getting a carbon monoxide protector? The thing you cannot see that kills and sneaks up on you and do you harm! So do not get caught off guard if you have signs. It is like warnings from the Lord to protect family. And this isn't the street stuff that isn't taught in church all the time or maybe it's rushed through like a water fall that makes it hard to catch the messages.

If we have the spirit of eternal life in us doesn't it make sense to protect it as much as possible? One of the biggest problems with the things that are going on with the government is they are in a spiritual warfare their egos are so far up in a state of cloudiness they do not know how to fight and find the right way out of themselves!

We all Matter

The way the state of the so-called leaders who are responsible for the country are performing and what kind of example they are setting that upsets the status quo, as well as their personal relationship with friends. The fact is there is lots of negative energy that is flowing over the atmosphere in the USA. That is why we need to raise ourselves up and others about it with love and know we can dismiss it out of our personal atmosphere with the love of the Lord. This can help to bring a balance of wanting to live and keep one's self safe from death.

Now the peer pressure is one other thing to be taught about to not let affect you that information comes in one of the books.

How do we look at the kaleidoscope of knowledge? It is like a vault that has been opened up to the conscious state of mind on a new level that has been sealed off from mankind. At the same time, it gives a way to a healthier environment within a state of love.

It is still for individuals to pass their own judgment on whether they believe or not in this as truth or a light out of a part of darkness.

The celebration of black history month gives lots of meaning to people who have an understanding of love in their heart. For some, there is so much hatred for one another that keeps them blinded and at the drop of a dime they kill one another.

It is not with honor that I see us as a people who are lacking in wisdom. It shows throughout the whole country. Now what can be done to turn this around? The power to excel to not stay blind and that only comes from truth.

To help stop the annihilation of young black men, get a plan! This is one to help keep us from perishing. A key to open the mind to put actions in line with the power of love can defeat the enemy inside of the lost or blind and bring into sight the freedom from a kind of bondage labeled as bola-bola. To gain the self-control that is needed get a copy of the book, _Why Do Black Men Harm Each Other more than Others?_ It gives understanding of the real cause and cure.

It has gotten to the point where there are too many people who are too busy trying to earn a living to understand the gift they have.

The New Attitude or Mindset

To learn to become content being a butcher, a baker
or candlestick maker there are too many expectations
put on the youth today to become a doctor, lawyer,
accountant or someone who is on a high level of pay.
That is unrealistic for some because they do not have
that kind of dream or desire to do things like that. That
is why you as adults should never try to live your
dreams through a child of yours. It will keep them
uncomfortable in ways it shouldn't.

All you need to let them know is to try to find
something to keep you happy and do it for a living. It
is better than being stressed out and somewhat out of
your true content of well being. Besides, it is always
better to live with less if you can gain more with a
peace of mind. That is a key to happiness. To be able
to give a presence of self-love is priceless and all the
wealth in the world can't buy it nor is it one of the
things you can take with you when you leave earth.

Youth need help to understand why they are having
so many problems. One reason is the towerists who
are in control of politics who are bought by lobbyists
who have gun control.

You can learn about the spirit man you have without
being any kind of genius. The only requirement is to
put on a common sense halo so you can see the light
in front of you without blinders on. They can only be

taken off with a heart-felt message that peace be with you and it radiated out of you not war, as some of the youth have been given out in the country at school.

It is time to stop the madness that leads to insanity and let the love shine out of people like it was meant to be.

Get this book to help prevent a possible crook from stealing its way out of you.

No Complications at all

Most people don't know what the meaning of love is and why it was created. The first thing is it is to be shared. The next thing; it is for the protection of people.

Not healthy

It is a problem that too many people start off thinking. It is a thing between two people. If you get hurt by it, it may take a bigger hit but it is not exactly that at all. It is at times the furthest thing that is going on between two people. Now two joined together is great but to get the most out of love you have to love the Lord and you first.

That is right, God created it to share it. He never had to go as far as sharing it, to the point his only son had to die on the cross in order for him to share his personality with us as if he had not done enough for us.

Next, there was a curriculum put together to teach us the next level of love. God knew it was the best ever because of all the other people who wanted to share in his love, dying on the cross. He could have in so many other ways showed his love. What God did himself to show and let the world know that the written word had life in it was died for us. It is to protect you from self, first of all, then anything else that thinks it can stop you from getting to heaven to be with the one and only God because of the faith you have in him.

Let's look at what it cost compared to what was paid for it. If you have any sense there is no comparison. Now who is given a chance to be smart? You of course.

If we don't know yet what love was created for as the Lord's son was also, then read this as many times as it takes to make sure you know your life may depend on it and know the Lord loves you. Now what is our biggest job in life helping people know the love of the Lord as well as how to use the wisdom of the freedom that goes along with it?

To be without these two things it is like a big level of poverty. The next is not being able to afford to take care of your daily needs housing, food and other things. But all of the needs can be met once you have not let yourself get shortchanged on the growth of love in your life even if it is only self-love to start.

A shortcut to victory

What will or what may be never understood is some people carry so much hate in their hearts that is buried so deep it doesn't want to come out. It is that kind of dislike for life that is poison. Only God can lay his breath of freedom on it. So if anyone feels so bad about their life ask the Lord for his breath of freedom. Say I need the break of freedom Lord for as long as you feel bad in order to protect yourself and others.

One of the keys to public safety can be found in *The New Added Protection for Teens and Young Adults at Risk*. If the Lord challenges you to do something why not at least try? Do you need to try this book? *How to Live With Less and Gain More*.

This can be known as the "read your way out of problems institution.

I am not being serious enough or strong with the intent to learn to protect myself or I am unhappy. This state of life can open the door for the void-noid, numb-dumb, sin-drome. You let them in the door. The two, or more, enemies can be defeated.

Big News

There is a cry for attention that so many youth are in need of and we have come up short. It is time to show them the love they are lacking that can be supplied to them. It is the love that they have down inside that the negative circumstances of life is burying on a daily basis. That must be changed.

We as adults are responsible to revive this part of the human existence. The technical age of life has replaced the innocent part that needs to be put back in place. It will do a world of good for them.

The plan uses God's brain surgery

The plan makes the spirit right so the mental will help correct itself. If you don't know the Lord's way is or may be the only way. It is time to know the right kind of spiritual health practice will help fix mental health. This is the food this is the nourishment that is needed to help make the change. But it is about it no backing out of it if we want to get it right so we sleep better at night.

A Chance to Change

Do we stay as if we are some kind of oxymoron that is apparently contradictory terms appear in (a) conjunction (e.g., faith but unfaithful (that) keeps (the) himself inside of you falsely true). Chop it up to make sense. If people keep doing the same thing in a way that may get little result to make themselves feel good it is okay but if people want better results and are presented with them but won't try the new way of doing something, then should they call themselves a kind of oxymoron? Or do they put on a blindfold to cover their mind, soul, body, eyes and spirit man and think everything will be alright or it is because I have made an offer and that is it takes from me.

I say if this is the case, there is some real soul searching that needs or must be done because this is only a shallow way of thinking and this process of growth takes us to get deeper than the human mind can think. Therefore, be in the know and don't leave yourself out because if you do you may be leaving out others.

This teaching can be considered the Olympics of spiritual growth where all are winners. It takes a desire and the Lord will do the best in show you the rest of what may be needed in your life to add to it.

To not make light of the fact that this violence has not been a problem in the spiritually endowed schools that have some kind of biblical teaching and that is the component that may be keeping them safe. That is why we need to introduce some kind of good news to them not being a specific religion just some spiritual skills.

People have done the thing like Jimmy Stewart but like in the movie it was the blessing from the Lord through the people that helped make things right. That is where we are to know the Lord gives us a way out of darkness in time so we can create a lighthouse, the traditions of people going to Washington. It is good though now it is time to go to God or let him come to you. That is the better way to get things done to learn to teach there are over 40 books that can help bless the people around the world.

Time is of the essence. We can help stop these kinds of problems from moving forward at Bound to Heaven Publishing/Ministries. The cries of the youth have been heard. It will be reckoned with now. It is also up to us to not let anyone slip or fall through the cracks. If we do, the blame is also on us. Right is fair and just not to just pass the buck.

In ending this chapter of understanding I open the new treaty that is a gift from the Lord to also save a part of humanity and it may be the one you love also. I hope the youthfulness does not see anything other than the love in this message from a messenger of the Lord, because I love you in Jesus' name.

To add this up as a nation we go and look to Washington to get answers. Now Washington is looking for us to give answers back. Like JFK said we should not ask what the country can do for you but what you can do for your country. We can make it as right as can be if we keep we together.

I want you to learn more than enough to weather any storm. So go as if your life depends on it to the books that will guarantee that you will not be confused about what it is time for you to know. The life substance of the most important part of the real DNA that is love, can now be lifted to a presence to stop the madness that leads to sadness in the places that are to be known as the third house of God. The first church, second home, third school.

We make these truths evident that the lamb's blood of the blessings shall protect all within and you that choose to do harm will be committing one's self to a hellish effect in reality. You shall travel that road alone. It has been written and it shall be known.

There is something that has been placed on the minds of people throughout history. The spiritual war of Armageddon that will come has put the world on a pathway that deep down inside has an effect of we all are living on the edge. But can we handle it? Yes, the preaching and teaching says that the world will end as we know it. With this being how it will take place. Does this fact affect people? Yes, in different ways, some good some not so good. We should all know that what man meant for evil, God can mean for good. That is why we put Satan on notice. This is an indictment on Satan in the court of justice. He has been evicted from the state of affairs that he has resided over mankind with.

You can find your way into the kingdom building Body of Christ right where you are at this moment today. I say this in the name of Jesus. There is a book that can cover every inch of what is written on this you can find in the website boundtoheaven.org and learn more about the house of God that is close to you. If you don't want to go there you would at least be introduced to the Ecumenical House of God Without Walls which is the foundation of Bound to Heaven Publishing/Ministries where you can find your way into the kingdom building Body of Christ.

The garden that God gives to mankind can be eaten from if you know the proper way to prepare a meal. There have been people who have been preparing meals who were supposed to have come from the Lord but did not.

In the cyber world where there is darkness there is a lot of food that has been prepared that is unhealthy, such as the eports that gamers use to feed people off of. Now what needs to take place is there has to be a botbuster to be put in place to stop this new portal that is spewing venom and disease. We can achieve this through an understanding that mankind gets that develops from his spirit-man within that can start off with a Little Mr. Fix-A-Thought in action that can be known as the Lord's therapy helper that uses spiritual skills. To stop the intruder that has been put in place in the atmosphere that is utilized through the worldwide web.

To know the wisdom of the Lord is the best journey you can have yourself adorned with. Find the knowledge and information to add all of this up that is being presented. Take your mind off this with more than one way to increase successful living with one of the formulas for success that will automatically take you there.

We must learn how to exercise our spiritual skills to a level as a part of our life skills are done. It is a part of the lifetime growing process that has not been tapped into much other than church or catholic school or a theological institution.

We are in need of the presence of these new kinds of spiritual skills put into mainstream society to keep a better balance of people who are in a troubled state that they may find themselves on a seemingly lonely pathway that can feed them spirituality that adds to faith and happiness. That can mean the world is a better place until they are better.

A hypothetical question that should not exist

Is there a dark side of some people who hate to get old and try to die young? If so, are there any distinctions of who they are? Or is this just another way to get a chance to play in hell? If there is, do we who make things worse in the eyes sick by having too much love showing but not sharing it helps push others off the deep end of life to a place where there is no coming back from they think for no thanks to be able to say thanks for love?

Let's keep it real: the Lord has many ways to get people started on a pathway to his teaching that can be acquired. I would not give anyone anything I cannot share without saying it has not been a blessing to me also.

That is why I can say to know that the Lord loves you enough that he wants you to know him,IT can be one of the best blessings to receive. So I write to show you how to know him better, because when you do this, you get to know yourself better. So many people need to know themselves better. That will make the world a better place. This is a part of what life is all about because the Lord is made up of and from love. Go to my website and dig into some of his love.

Can you see the blue wings on your back? I can!

Who is it that got game when white men learn how high they could jump? Black men still won't jump off a mountain with a pair of skies or parachute or glider. I say this to tell you that the most important stockholders of this land call America have not been pleased at the way it has been used up and inhabited by just about all people in one way or the other. The more wicked you are the more you have harmed it.

So I will go with not using your resources in keeping it clean and/or just wasting the natural resources. We need to be more mindful of the people who really own this place in the first place. Now, that it is just on loan to us as humans in a state of visiting hear the planet earth.

The real sky chief disciples were here thousands of years ago. To be truthful, we should feel blessed by them and the almighty that we can be a part of the company of people who are the angels' marshals of the sky. To do this thing with leaving the earthly body at the same time is a real honor. Special thanks to the teachers that are in the sky already waiting to show us a better way to love.

I have been thinking and I feel we should put some new guardians and new wise men in place or kind of watchmen for the Lord in addition to the disciples. They are needed to watch the backs of the earthlings to be able to get to the level of sky chief disciples.

I believe the more we add to the roll that takes care of not just the country but the world, the better we can get along and do the right thing when we see something that must be stopped.

This all around process may become a new way of life. Once you get going doing what you like and, when needed, become a kind of spiritual hero that God sends on missions to help people in need with his love that is expressed in the best ways possible.

I had a need to stop bullying in my neighborhood. Once I was going to do harm to someone but someone else got to him before I got there. Thank God I didn't have to have that on my conscience.

Time Out

If you think you are crazy it is okay I did somewhat at one time and before I know it the Lord lets me work the crazy out of me, on a job and inside of my head and my writing helps me do it. Now it may be good therapy for you to ask the Lord to give you a way to do the same.

Some people in my neighborhood though I had a problem and was kind of crazy but it can't bother you if you know like I did. It was not all the way true but a part of it was. Now I learned after I got older it may have been lead poisoning that contributed to it.

We make better news

Can we use something better than the gut feelings to announce some kind of warning? What can be better? The spiritual eye that sees through darkness. This new intervention takes place only because of the growing level of spiritual skills. They will develop as you share and grow the love inside of you.

We are able to level with a new kind of social endeavor once we change the towerism from the ruling powers in government the vote will take them out, to start that will put us on the road to a happier nation, like New Zealand.

This can be worth more than all the gold in the world to have a happy nation. We can live longer, cut down on so much violence and harm plus crime; the list is endless. This is how the youth can help make the future better as they grow up into it. The ball is really in your court more than anyone. It is an undertaking to be proud of and it should be shared as much and as often as could be.

This can help keep the human race on a greater level than can be talked about all of the time because showing it beats telling it in ways that life is to be enjoyed. If you have not learned the best way to help to keep yourself happy is to keep the children of the world safe and happy. It should also be a goal of everyone in the world. There should be no greater sacrifice than ones made for the children.

Today, learn the facts about when people are not smart enough to avoid something in their pathway, they run into it. Ask how many people get things put in their pathway. That is right and one of the biggest things that gets in the way of growth is the void-noid numb-dumb sin-drome. It is the negative part of life people run into sometimes for no apparent reason or fault of their own, from being naïve just because they are trying to find a way to go in life that will show them who they are. They may become someone who they are not that may take something out of them or growing pains to get away from.

What is the point? Whether you went there or you need to avoid going there. The teaching of spiritual skills is to help you get out or stay away. That is why it is so important. It is one of the biggest survival tools on the planet to get protected from the void-noid, numb-dumb, lame-duck, sin-drome (and you if need be).

One or more of the reasons people get out of line with themselves is they do not want to know themselves, or they do not know themselves, or they do not want to know who they have become, or who they will become. What can anyone do about this temporary odyssey? Pray to know who the real you is and deep down inside you are just like most people, a good person who may have gotten caught up in the void-noid, numb-dumb, lame-duck, sin-drome state that can be an inherited trait or innocent mistake but from where it came or was developed, it can be eliminated with spiritual skills.

The negativity of euphoria is like an addiction that can wear off. However, if it is too wreckless, someone can get hurt. That is not a part of the life anyone wants. That is why intervention is needed.

To whomever sees this in their heart, I am a somewhat nobody. I have been largely ignored by the public at large. Can someone stop and see what I have been doing with my life to show the love I have?

The New Added Protection for the Development of Teens and Young Adults at Risk is a kind of before therapy to stop the problem of violence at school from happening and an after the fact therapy, if this happens again. The harming of a student at any school that I have the greatest of hope that it will not happen again. This is why I hope everyone in America is exposed to this message with the teaching it possesses.

The new added protection can help provide the power of spiritual skills pre-awareness crisis intervention therapy before and after. Try the new guidelines for helping to keep the youth safe.

This is an invitation to become
a part of the spiritual skills revolution

It is the thing of the future don't be late. This may be a program to get with the help to bring some new blessings in your life. To be known I feel good about the fact that every book I have written have the elements of spiritual skills in them for all to know.

Does the reason for 99% of school shootings come from males have something to do with these facts? The boys' masculinity has been dethroned in ways that have had so many of mankind thinking like they are alienated to not see the sensitivity of femininity in conjunction with masculinity being unbalanced.

There is too much self-expectation that does not have the true understanding of the limitations of love which can work outside of one's self. This is hard in today's society for some. The displacement comes into a dark side when the harmony of peoples' ability to reflect and think outwards is not there. Refrain from doing something stupid: resist, recognize and don't regurgitate evil to come out on someone else.

To end the final state of a tomb that is out of tune people need the right spiritual growth. Look at it any way you wish. It will all boil down to that because where there is no spiritual growth present people are out of tune and touch.

To make it plain, spiritual skills can be considered God's cure for a superbug. This cure is put to work to stop the void-noid, numb-dumb, lame-duck, sin-drome. It can make people aware of almost anything negative that wants to hide in an evil, harmful, non-seen and destructive force that may happen that may try to sneak up on someone.

This can be considered information to detect the white side of darkness that exists that is not right. It cannot be seen by eyesight but it is known to exist. The Lord's cure for the superbug identifies it so you can reject it.

This process works on all levels where there may be an intruder. There are no if's and's or but's about it. It is my hope that you have the answers to any questions you have anticipated, if you think you want to learn it from the writings I have done. I also hope it answers the one question that shows us how to come together, as was meant to be, being the most diversified mix of people the earth will ever know.

We can learn how to minimize the harm that this new kind of cold warmongers cause. We can do one thing; come back together. They cannot slip into our mindset with their dark invader status. They use tools like the worldwide web for us to not be an open society. We need to protect ourselves against them from weaponizing us against ourselves. That is what spiritual skills, which we have can do. Others may be jealous about this, possibly through no fault of their own.

Satan has his way of pitting powers against one another. That is why we are forgiven because we learn from our mistakes even if someone else causes them. Now we can try to teach other countries how to love more. It might open the door for us to have more love for ourselves in America.

The real part of the downfall is when someone can't find a way out of themselves. In other words, they get lost and somewhat locked inside in a tomb-like non-realistic state that leaves them emotionless, possibly experiencing paranoia and schizophrenia. Depression also kicks in and the mental state of the welfare is subject to a breakdown. In some cases they turn around and try to break out of life. With a last ditch effort they get with Satan to become a coward and want others to go with them. If Satan is not on his job, then I might as well not have written this at all.

To keep it moving, as it is shown time and time again, family members harm the family when it is as the brother who killed his sister and niece. To keep it moving, the disgruntled employee killed the people at the job. Now let's look over all killings and we find a road that leads back to greed, haterism or simply not enough love. All are symptoms of void-noid, numb-dumb, lame-duck, sin-drome and Satan is backing all of them.

Break down a problem and look inside. If you need help get it but if more people put Dr. God's therapy with whatever else is needed, there would be a whole lot less sickness on a mental/spiritual or spiritual/mental presence on earth.

One of the biggest assistants you have to help you work through the bad weather inside or outside of you is to talk to someone. Don't keep things bottled up inside you and let them fester. It can become a blister where puss will develop in you and poison you.

If you deny yourself now you will appreciate it later!

Beware of sexting. It is a promiscuous thing. It is time to stop this if you are doing it. If you are not doing it, don't start. It is a member of Satan's workshop of tools and his way to get to hard headachers. I say this because a bad kind of habit can be formulated out of what may seem like a fun and cute thing that can alleviate or escalate to another kind of darkness. don't play with this kind of fire. It can burn with the devastating tragedies that can come along with it in ways that may harm someone's dignity or moral principles of life. Sex talk is not a thing you need to be toying around with. Whether you can believe it or not, it can be like a loaded gun that people are playing Russian roulette with. It also has the power to harm.

To not know all the rules that go along with the issue of sex on a level is an immature thing that a young person should not do. It could start what could be a good game that has consequences that some people are not equipped to face with many additional pressures that go along with it.

The truth is, there are bad habits that can formulate with the so-called innocent game of sex talking. It is also harming adults. It may have been prevented if they had enough of a warning to not make light of the issues of sex, on any level, or of attracting fun to it without the right level of maturity.

Don't open Pandora's Box because the tools of Satan are in there that don't need to be touched. When the time is right get the blessings of the Lord to really enjoy the intimacy that doing the right thing can offer.

Why ask why? I will tell you why. All people are blessed with the Lord's grace and some people still may seem like they are not. We see the harm that people in other countries are experiencing, being killed and suffering. It is not right and we should know that we are not any better than them in the sight of the Lord. Why this is I don't know exactly but we are to become our brothers' keeper in the Body of Christ. However, I believe someone is not doing their job. It is pure evil that has taken over a place where someone is harming others like they are not human and they will answer for that. The innocent, when they are killed, get a ticket to heaven.

On the other side, as in the USA, if someone is not totally covered by the understanding of their grace it too is like an enemy is in the camp of their well-being to live a peaceful life. They will be disturbed, tried and tested. This is because Satan's job is to steal you away from under the grace of the Lord. Once that starts to take place, it becomes harder and harder at times to get back home with the Lord because he resides in your heart. That is why the part in life called religious fellowship is a way that people go in to get a specific placement of people of their likeness.

Spiritual learning is on many levels and it can multiply the grace that you have if need be. This blocks, knocks and takes Satan out of the mix that may be going on in your head. It is enough to keep the norm at bay and move forward in life without the devil in his details inside of someone's mind. This will add the unnecessary pressure and temptation of acting out ugly showing how Satan has become a part of your life. He is ruling in darkness.

We can stop this madness that leads to sadness and death with the vision of the Lord that is in every man's heart. It can be touched by all no matter who you are and where you are. Satan is dead and the Lord is alive. Amen and Hallelujah

Do the frog

If you think you are stuck in the fog, take a leap up to the sky to see the sunroof that the Lord's son supplies. The sun of the Lord that is always attached to you with his invisible umbilical cord. It is always there not like the one from your mother that has been separated so you can stand on your own feet. Take a leap with your faith to protect yourself, even from you if need be. Stay alive to watch you strive for the height that love will bring you even if you go through a storm.

I Could, I Should, I Will

I could, but I shouldn't talk about my endless days and nights.

I could, but I won't talk about my tireless efforts to find the right way to go.

I could, but I won't tell of the depths of hell I have been in.

I could, and I will show you the love that was given to my life from God and His children.

I Could, I Should, I Will

Spiritual skills are to help scare away what could be a demon thinking process. Some people may go as far as wanting some kind of exorcism that doesn't seem to be in any way real.

What we are doing at Bound to Heaven Publishing/Ministries is dusting off the old news and polishing off the things that are more precious than gold, such as the greatest umbilical cord of the Lord. It can only be cut or severed at the gates of hell.

When the baby's cord was cut from the mother at birth it gave Satan a way to attach itself and perpetrate that the Lord's umbilical cord got cut also. That is deception and trickery. So people can fool themselves to think the Lord has left them at times that may be hard on them, but no way does the Lord leave you.

The human mind will always air to the negative because of fear. But when you do the things that you fear then the death of it comes along. We can rise up.

Neverness is fear all balled up. Neverness can keep you moving forward instead of fear that keeps you standing in one place to be approached by the void-noid, numb-dumb, lame-duck, sin-drome. We kicked to the curb what holds us back. Break the Geronimo curse of the things that keep you down. It is successful living that may be looked at as the same way, no money that keeps you in poverty. They are the same just on two levels. The wealthiest people in the world are problems solvers.

Now you have just become a problem solver and the wealth you now possess is to not remain in a state of spiritual poverty in life.

You have been approved to move up in the world and enjoy life at the very stage you are at. Your opportunities are expanding daily.

As two may be

It is not all the time that a great messenger can be a great writer. To whom much is given, much is still required.

Time End

We finally made it to the point where we have put enough data together along with the facts. We can now provide a prediction of how and why people snap out of control.

These are the preventive measures that have been put together to analyze the occurrence of negativity that responds with the reaction everywhere on the planet creating harm to others. This is a calculated pattern of prediction that has the analytical data of prediction. It can be headed off to stop it from happening by way of exposing the truth about it and its cause and its cure.

The more who knows the less it will show up again. This increases the best way to stop violence at school, home, etc. breaking a code that mankind has been in the dark or silent about.

The things that have been in the dark are starting to come to light in many ways that are needed by mankind. This law of average has reached this stage of growth principles. It is about the science of living that has a way of examining itself, then presenting itself with the blessings of the Lord that goes along with it.

This book is for anyone who wants to kill at school and then some; age doesn't matter. Now if you feel bad about the school example tell someone at home a parent, guardian or if not talk to a teacher or counselor.

The Lord has commissioned this book as a way to help stop school shootings.

To help take your mind off of yourself and your problems, think about the fact that our country is in crisis and you and others like you can do something about it.

Now is the time to "x" out the psychology of pysche of the fairytale on when Satan keeps the people lost in the pysche of what the people think is the problem. It is not; it is lost out of spirituality.

John O'Neil predicted that the foreign enemy would do something. The FBI was all over the place and they didn't get along with him all the way. The CIA had a problem with him and after his 25 year war ended with the FBI, they said he had to go. Two weeks after he started at the twin towers job, the planes hit. He knew something was going to happen but only put together a part of it.

The facts are in. look at what you are learning and help the country get it right. It is the underlying problem that is getting fixed first. This is an agreement to control your narrative.

The sole purpose of the books is the tools are made available to teach people how to become faith healers to themselves. They can teach a nation how to heal itself. I personally claim no victory that what is done for you is by my hand. It is by the Lord's hand that the victory is made with your faith.

I wish I had more of the love that the late departed Billy Graham had for people. I do in a way that only God knows at the time I wrote this, I mourn his passing as if he was as close to me as an earthly relative. I would love to be the kind of man as I believe he was.

I had a visit on March 2nd from Dr. Billy Graham. His spirit man talked to me and told me to keep the work up and keep the faith. Through the ministry I have been given to shepherd over the ecumenical house of God without walls I evangelize to more people so they know that the Lord keeps his promises. I try to let people know the Lord does not want this great nation of Americans to become separated. It is to be a landmark for the love of the Lord for all the world to see and know. It must get back on course or it will not become this place where there could be great miracles performed.

I believe Billy Graham wanted to pass a part of the gift to others before he left. I thank him and the Lord for him.

Spiritual skills helps increase the big 4 to defeat depression. Spiritual skills is a killer because it increases Dopamine, Serotonin, Oxytocin, Endorphins.

The looming tower to review a political drama that actually has something to say. Al-Qaeda and the road, Lawrence Wright author, Publisher Alfred A. Knopf.

The strange thing is it seems like the Rev. Billy Graham needed to let me know to keep doing what I am doing and it seems like he passed me a staph or some kind of stick that could have been a baton.

This is a process of thinking I will try to share with you so we can stop the spiritual death from the dead. The American Revolutionary War, The Civil War, The Blue Suits, WWI, WWII, the end of 1864, the beginning of 1780-1863 ,blacks seeking freedom, the major fights took between 1619 and 1865 that started on the war ships. Were we the last to come around from home warring? I think so.

We can't be defined by fake news;
only what is real will last forever

First of all, this is not just a book. It is a road map that has been developed by a spirit-man guide. This has been done in order for the youth to know that we are depending on them more than ever to get ahead of the problem that our country is facing.

It is not a pretty picture that has been happening. The spirit of America has been broken to a level that has put a damper and drain on the lives of many people, especially the young people of all cultures. To add to it, the actions that have made a generation to be looked at as if they are lost.

The new evangelists are being sent out from the calling of the Lord to take a hand to show love and to not let the nation get into a spiritual warfare within the country itself. The steps have been taken and put into place. All you have to do is show up with your faith. It will be one of the greatest building blocks we as a people can use in the future. I hope to see you on the front line.

We the people, can write the greatest part of American history for the next 1,000 years if we become the nation that we were meant to be. The Lord has plans for us. Will we take our time to get to know them? Will we throw them out with the trash and let the nation be turned into trash? It is up to the few to guide us all in the right direction. The Lord knows your heart can change but do you? If not, it is time to pick up your cross and follow him.

I don't know exactly when I started but by the time I was 13-14 yrs. old, I was on my way. It seemed like I ran into some of my most difficult times, but I kept going. It still doesn't feel like I have conquered all I need to but I give you a part of my faith now to add to yours to help. I hope you get further than I may get with mine.

So it is written now let it be told; don't be afraid to receive your blessings at any age. It is the Lord's love that will carry you through it all until the very beginning. It never ends and you better believe that.

This is the pathway to freedom for billions of people. God's spirit bots will stop Satan in his tracks. They will turn him around with no place for him to go but down.

I will give you a few scenarios. At the White House there is a tower of power called Donald Trump. Now when a tower is getting cleaned out, as he has done in the past, they slip out the waste, which in a tower's case is bricks. On their way down out of a window they hit people upside or on top of their head. How many can you count that have gotten hit from the tower fallout? All he is going to do will still be reverberating and will come to a head about 7 years from 2018, along with other processes that have to be subdued in a Godly manner.

How many more will be hit and that is just the ones in the White House? We look at the country and without making as estimate we want to take it to another kind of level. The so-called big house has trouble in it and it creates planet warfare. This negative energy is given to Satan and he spreads it out to the land. Who suffers? The people, from the spiritual warfare that rains down on them from the fallout from the crash.

To see and not say is the worst thing people can do but to not see and can't say is even worst. That is what we do as messengers. Now we move on and say the young man who killed 17 people in Florida had a sickness. Did Satan have anything to do with it? Heck yes, because the sickness was of an evil nature. If it just was of a mental problem people could have worked with him but when Satan hides the evil in a high dark place in some people it takes the gift of the discernment of the spirit in people, we need more people to be able to do this.

Getting to the point, we can get people to open up to us by the sight they show. We can know to help stop this problem. It may rain down even more in the days to come if we don't get ahead of it.

Do you see the connection of the way Satan can work and then the mental process that we all have to work our way through? At times we cannot be harmed by the spiritual sickness that are treated with spiritual skills.

As for the latest young man who killed his parents in Michigan, I have not learned much about it. It could have been a slap upside the head state of evil where Satan had a chance to hurt the killer that wasn't meant to happen. Any way you look at it, it was madness out of control.

A gun put together, is the devil's workshop. People who don't have the skills needed to work their way out of Satan's boot camp don't need to be in this kind of position ever. The loved one they have gets hurt and they have pain behind this also. That is why the void-noid, numb-dumb, lame-duck, sin-drome has a lock on it to not enter with the use of the SSS (super spiritual skills) that are stronger than Satan's traps. It has been made somewhat clear drugs may have been what incited him into killing his parents.

To be clear what do we do to help stop what could be the next war on American soil? It is the stopping of the gun culture cold war. It has been developing in ways that can only be fueled by Satan.

The homes of America are so full of it. Where it is present is not to be believed. That is why it is not talked about. People don't need to get any more paranoid or apprehensive about it, but soon many people are running on overload with their emotions and this must decrease. Thank God we are aware of this so we don't add to it.

What we have to look at is the truth. It is crazy to a certain measure that so many people have so many weapons. There is a silver lining: with spiritual skills it is possible to maintain a quiet and normal state of mind. If they all got hit with so much crap and the demons of darkness kick in, the state of our country would look like it did in the Civil War and worse.

That is the truth. God has better things he wants us to do with our life and time. Besides, the whole world is waiting to see how we get out of this temporary mess we are in and let's do this for peace. God would be so proud of us. There is not a thing wrong with giving gifts to loved ones in heaven. I give to my mother lots because if it wasn't for my parents, I would have not become the man I am.

As a majority, we can defeat the prejudices that cause discrimination against ethnic or racial groups of all people. It is Satan's plan to try to do a Charles Manson on a sea of people that put them up in arms against one another. His goal is to remove civility from the free world and to have people commit genocide against one another anywhere he can. That doesn't exclude Americans if he can get his plan to work.

Look at what is happening in other parts of the world. If you see what I see, it is because of a few factors. The biggest one is towerism and it is time out. This can be stopped.

We can help. Read the books I have put together to defeat the power that Satan has been using over the world to harm people. You can learn to help stop it. By the time 2025 gets here we should have defeated this evil presence in this lifetime. Besides, who, with an ounce of sense, wants to be a part of self-destruction?

The Lord has a plan and it is time to present it to the generations that he has chosen. It wasn't meant for the generations before or the generations after you. It was meant for you to be the ones that bring forth this message to love God, thy neighbor and thy country as never before.

American Creed

"I believe in the United States of America as a
government of the people, by the people, for the
people; whose just powers are derived from the
consent of the governed, a democracy in a republic, a
sovereign Nation of many sovereign States; a perfect
union, one and inseparable; established upon those
principles of freedom, equality, justice, and humanity
for which American patriots sacrificed their lives and
fortunes.

I therefore believe it is my duty to my country to love
it, to support its Constitution, to obey its laws, to
respects its flag, and to defend it against all enemies."

Pledge of Allegiance

"I pledge the allegiance to the flag of the United of
America and to the Republic for which it stands one
nation under God indivisible with liberty and justice for
all."

Repeat this over and over know this and soul and
stand for it daily.

We should be aware that we will have wars coming at
us in at least two ways or more the good thing is we
can use our foresight to get ahead of things. Now if
you think this is too much for you and you are too

young. It is understandable the USA is not like Pakistan were kids 10 to 12 use weapons on civilians.

To the youth: know that when things in life hit you low, you come back high on a better level of love for all mankind. This is standard procedure for growth. God speed to all. From a servant of the people in the name of the Lord.

A big part of all people's lives is they all need connections so how much is the question for you to know?

Let's try to take this perspective: if two states of growth are in an objectivity of the other one, can we have a clear finding of an irregular pattern of development as the mental clashes with the spiritual process? It does not happen to all people. Could it cause a problem of added depression or schizophrenia?

I look at this as a possible problem. Could pregnant mothers help to avoid this possible issue in the future of a human with spiritual enhancement as the child develops in the womb? Just a thought.

Can this be a way to calm the lack of development of a hypothesis to back things up that came upon some of the human race?

All of the work I do is a part of God's special weaponry that isn't a secret weapon. You can consider it a part of the towering down movement.

This is energy at its best. It can reproduce the needs of some with the helping hand of their development of love. It is in truth and pure power to be shared. This helps people get out of the chaos that some go through that they seem to get lost in their universe of their inner hemisphere.

This is a healthcare system that is also needed to bring new life to life that is off track in life.

The side that needs to be known

When things go down and some become lost they will or might have to pay a personal cost. All of what may become yocky-dock that is talked about all over the place will have to not be placed in the reality of life. Now we can protect ourselves and others from the brain-freezes and block outs from blackouts of thoughts that push people into the void-numb, numb-dumb, lame-duck, sin-drome place of hopelessness thanks to the Lord.

This is the development of a new process that is being put in place to stop the intruders that have been infiltrating the country through the worldwide web. This process of eliminating them can be labeled as the dee da-da dee process that can stop ongoing violence on a spiritual plane or playing field that comes by way of the computer. In retrospect looking at the bullying phase that takes place, the process consists of every time you find negativity you start off with the dee da-da dee put whatever negative message there is so people can be aware of it. Then end the message again with dee da-da dee stop the madness and the poison.

This is the code of the sky chief disciples

God's dots reveal a part of the bad spots in life

We have three phases of possible negative growth that we have to be prepared to eliminate from society. The first one is the government that we live under. The second one is outside of the country enemies. The third one is personal defaults that we are not supposed to inherit. This is a way to not let the three strike rules put us out of life's mainstream of growth. To be clear, spiritual skills cut out the mishegoss-meshugaas.

The insincere spiritual feedback comes by way of the reminiscent state of memory helps you in developing the keys to love.

Let the Lord do the thinking

Take note; there have been three great awakenings that were put before the people. If there is a fourth one, the Lord wants you to be prepared. I do not think I can predict the coming of anything but the Lord knows. He said he would come back and I believe in him and his word.

I will say the part that I feel good about is the 144,000 that will be caught up to be a part of the new kingdom. The part that I am excited about is I may have something to do with the teaching of one or more of them since I have been fulfilling my calling to teach the gospel of Christ in the way in which the Lord has called me. Furthermore, you may be a part of that also because you are reading this now. Even if you are not one just by using what you have learned from the teaching at BTHPM, it will be credited to your account that you passed it along to some others in life.

Let's go there. How much do you want to be connected to the Lord? Are you just someone who wants to make it into heaven? That is all and not look for any work that relates to your gift. I did not at first when I started writing but soon I changed my mind. I stop fearing my skills. The first book had an idea that it would go to the place in which it has gone. It is like that with just about all the books I have been called to author. Forgive me if it seems like it has put you in an awkward position. It is the spiritual will in me doing what it does. Thank you for understanding.

I look back at the time I have invested in the work of the ministry I have been blessed to do. I see the one thing I now have trouble with. Have I done enough and could I have done more? The answer is yes. It does not sit well with me. I carry on and try harder every day to live up to the best I have to offer. Thank you for it is a blessing to me if anyone hears what I am writing about. This also goes for and to the "we" generation that I feel is taking charge in the right way.

Acts 2:17-20
17. And it shall come to pass in the last days, says God, that I will pour out of My Spirit on all flesh; Your sons and your daughters shall prophesy, Your young men shall see visions, Your old men shall dream dreams.
18. And on My menservants and on My maidservants I will pour out My Spirit in those days; And they shall prophesy.
19. I will show wonders in heaven above and signs in the earth beneath: Blood and fire and vapor of smoke.
20. The sun shall be turned into darkness, and the moon into blood, before the coming of the great and awesome day of the Lord.

Now do we hear?

Why didn't you obey my voice? The enemy is in your place and I cannot draw them out because you did not obey my voice. People: we do not want to fall under the label of the Lord saying you did not obey my voice. That is why we hear this message and are in action about our calling. This is the power of love that shines about us. Amen

Muse news

Never forget we were created to make the praise for the Lord glorious. I say again, I will bring glory to his name.

Muse news

To have a true spiritual nature gives you more than a reasonable benefit of having no doubt.

Billy Graham told me to carry out the ministry throughout the world. He also meant this for the "we people."

This is a pick me up moment

To the new millennials: this new book helps people get their lives back from where or what may have caused them to lose it. It is a process to bringing someone's courage back to the front of their lives that got left behind out of their lives.

To help stop the killing you as adults must stop over-coddling of a youth to a degree where they cannot see the forest for the trees in front of them. That is why there has not been any compassion for others when they see them in trouble.

They turn a blind eye to others in trouble because they are spoiled or want to be. Now is the time to give in to this generation of the youths that have to be the ones to bring a multitude to the forefront of their life.

In America, we have not had this happen in more than a two hundred year span, when some of the teens had to go to war but this is a different kind of war. It is a war of peace to stop a war on two fronts, spiritual and earthly.

If the Lord had not had me on my job, those days, weeks and months to put in place the safety measures of prevention, the outcome could have been of a different kind. Now, it is a horse of a different kind that wants to storm upon the land of America. It will take more than the tens of thousands I had to make aware. It will take millions of people to be aware. As the Lord took twelve and started what is a part of the mission he was on for the heavenly father, we must continue to grow and stay on course.

The spirit of the youths will have to be redeemed at a point we do not want to get lost out of control any further. If we look at other countries and see how their youth are made to grow up at a much earlier age in so many ways to sacrifice the way they need to be done is not so bad at all. It beats having them put a gun in their hand to defend themselves.

The Lord chose this country to show us how to put love in our minds, hearts and souls to conquer the wickedness that wants to defeat us. If it takes one, two or three generations of our youth to come together and grow in the power of love that will be shared all over the world, so be it in order to increase the Body of Christ that needs a new building platform. If this is a placement of healing the hearts and minds of mankind so let it be written, told and heard.

Keeping it real

"We people" need new eyes, new perspectives, and new objectives. "We people" are at a stage of growth in a way that history has never seen. It looks as if the government cannot help us take care of this thing we are facing. In a way, "we people" have to take care of the government until it can take care of itself again and only God knows when that will be. This is the bottom line so "we people," it is up to us to take care of home and turn this world around in a way that gives it a better outlook on humanity. All for one and one for all.

We are all the dreamers with the greatest capacity for love. It is time to set the stage to give heaven a show on how we people can let the devil pass us by and share it with the whole world in order for them to do the same in Jesus' name. "We people" are now the leaders of the best way to protect the government and the people in our land, no doubt about it. Thank God that someone can.

The chosen generation has become that way by no fault of their own. Take no offense, it is truly time to show up or shut up if you have not studied to show yourself to be approved by and in the will of the Lord. The presence of the state of omnipotence has also brought the omnipresence to a level of growth no other institution on earth can supply. It is a joint venture with the Lord and Holy Spirit to teach and equip the forerunners of daily events leading up to the presence of the coming of Christ and the denial of the Anti-Christ.

It is time for the building of a new government as the world stands and as the world will stand. Now do not think it is time for a state of Armageddon. It is a time to wake up every one that may be asleep. The "we people" have no fear because the Lord is here and near.

Treating childhood trauma

This can be considered revolutionary care. This is spiritual care. The process of this enlightenment can wipe the slate clean of childhood trauma.

I have been preaching this for years thanks to the Lord and have put this in the books I have authored. Have you had enough? Oprah said. We are on the verge of something big, this may be just that.

The "me" youth movement is today and happening now they have no set ups or set backs.

This is a part of the eternal guidance system that has been waiting for someone to set up the compass in order to know the right direction in which to go. It has now been presented to the "we people" who have been on a holding pattern. They are ready to move forward in the pursuit of happiness that will make this a better world.

The good part about this is, there is no initiation or requirement, only the belief in the power of love to start you on the road to create successful lives besides yourself. No one is excluded no matter the nationality, race or ethnic background. The label of prejudice does not exist in this presence of us because we are the just plain "we people."

The foundation's goal is for spiritual wellness all over the world to end prejudice on all levels with the sky being the limit. You can be a part of this or the ecumenical house of God without walls that has developed a way to make this world a better place. BTHPM works this plan with the sky chief disciples. This and all the projects are a dispensary of love and truth it is like having a medical exam that makes a house call at any time, any place. All you have to do is dial up the Holy Spirit to get the healing that you are in immediate need of. Then go for the follow up in the places you feel the need to and to the procedures.

It is nice to know we are all loved and that means you.

Open up

Thank you for your concern. If you are reading this book it shows that you are ready to be propelled into a new cavern in your mind to reach a galaxy of stars that creates an enchanting feeling of bliss. This is the presence of information that can reorganize a life to make it better. It is not to be confused with a group or someone that doesn't have a level of dominating a life but has to think for themself and be their own person. Besides, your time is precious since you may be learning how to be master of the universe that you have within to give back to people what they may be lacking that Satan has stolen.

You, You and You

The biggest thing I would love to see someone do is give the country, and the world, a greater understanding of what the love of the Lord is all about and how He helps people work things out and how he can help people prevent things from happening. This I believe can be done to stop the thief in ways that has never been done in the presence of mankind.

If someone takes the time to read most or all of the books I have written, it will be like a big baton or staph that someone will have to present to the world. The more that have one the better the world becomes. Then we can be really equipped and blessed even more at times when we are tried by Satan. Then the audience will get even larger as the people of heaven see how we caused the devil to pass us by.

The emptiness of the knowledge that is missing is a big problem. This can be fixed. Keep reading, you may be getting one of the best starts…

To prevent PTSD in the young people who have been at schools where violence has erupted spiritual skills will help. To the military, all four branches, spiritual skills will help. To all black youth who may be suffering from any kind of bola-bola, spiritual skills will help. That is a different kind of trauma that may lie in the genetic make up of a person. They may have a confused DNA that has adapted a negative trait of ungodliness. There are endless possibilities for advancement on all levels of life when someone includes spiritual skills.

Are there new levels of skills that need to be known spiritually? The un-gambling process of the life we have been given to make good on…by derailing the

void-noid, numb-dumb, lame-duck, sin-drome in order
not to let one's self be overcome by what will not
make sense no matter how it is twisted or turned.
Thank God for his foresight that can bring light to all
darkness that allows people to steer clear of troubles.

M-N

It is a big deal that too many people are losing the
light. It isn't right for anyone to lose their light line
because it is like a lifeline.

M-N

One of the most important things we do is teach
people what they need to have as a narrative to
speak into existence to educate them on how to make
it come to fruition. Sometimes they do not have to
understand it completely but it will help effect change.

Do not fool yourself

Do you know that if the Lord sends someone to you
and you are hating on them you are also hating on the
Lord in a subconscious way? How many people that
the Lord has doing something do you know about that
you do not like them or what they are doing? You
won't give them the time of day. Note: there is no
such thing as a little sin. There may be an unknown
sin that some people commit. But once you are aware

of it, it is what it is so show beats tell and no one can tell this on you but yourself.

If you are hating on anyone you are hating on the Lord. Take it for what it is worth. You may be decreasing your own self-worth. Believe that if you want to keep it real. Then pray for yourself to stop being an undercover hater, who is fake on the inside but has a smile on the outside.

The crazy part is I had to stop hating on people who were hating on me. It got to me because I had the spirit of discernment. I had to become the one who stopped throwing stones.

Warning

To anyone who cannot believe the truth when you hear it or are not able to accept it, you are a person who has been zombitized. That falls under the void-noid, numb-dumb, lame-duck, sin-drome. So look out for your next step into a kind of reality that can fulfilled: the step to being a full-fledged zombie.

Scroll No. II

What could be the underlying principle at BTHPM? It is the defeat of the army that Satan has. It is to find better ways to stop him from recruiting people. It is to get people to get a way (24/7) out of the presence of the rank and file. It is to dismantle the abilities to put together the needed people to make its storm hell-fires on a multitude of people. It is to weaken Satan's force and unveil the plan that he has set in place for thousands of years. It is to make believers out of anyone who do not believe that there is a God and he loves them. That could be one of the most important things of all.

This will increase the strength of kingdom building while we are still on earth. When we leave here we cannot do it in the flesh. But the footprints we leave behind can and hopefully will be the ones who are carrying someone off of the battlefield to freedom to be with the Lord.

2 Chronicles 7:14
14. If My people who are called by My name will humble themselves, and pray and seek My face, and turn from their wicked ways, then I will hear from heaven, and will forgive their sin and heal their land.

I had a bad experience when I was around two different dice games and one person got shot in the head. I was across the street but took off running like everyone else. I found out later he tried to resist the robber but did not make it. At another dice game someone got stabbed over cheating or not. It ended in another tragedy.

Even still, I knew people who were robbed and sold drugs. There was violence on both levels. This is not living. It is gambling with life. The fact that anyone who wants to do this has been affected by some kind of influence or trauma that caused them to have PTSD from some of OPP (other peoples' problems), that gave someone a bipolar disorder which made them develop trauma in their life. That made them act like a towerist of some kind who does not care about their fellow man on a moral level.

This is the sickness that keeps on giving until it is broken away from. The human kindness with understanding will help if you know what is happening that caused it and/or doing the self-awareness therapy. The spiritual skills teaching shows the person how to outgrow all of the issues in life with the strength of the Lord at their back pushing and pulling you up and away from a negative past.

Spiritual skills are act like a hate extinguisher. No matter how tough you are, if you put an open mind to work it will give you a chance to learn something new. This will un-skin the inner head that takes control of the fact that teaches people the right things to do whether they want to or not. It has the "I give up control" affect to allow doing what is good.

To clear things up even more the trauma toasting of a person can put, push and sink someone into a state that leaves them open to the void-noid, numb-dumb, lame-duck, sin-drome. That is the playground for Satan to plot the demise of someone in his disguised state until he is ready to pounce on them with pain and self-destruction of any kind.

Spiritual skills teach people how to have the right kind of conversation with themselves. After the fact of being trauma-toasted their brain is somewhat fried and the sin that has been developed on their spirit is starting to take away from their security or start to create insecurities. The hate-monger is awakened in them and a fight begins to wear on the human psyche. That labels them as enemy to themselves. They get lost out of the goodness that they should be possessing and bad thoughts pop up about them. A cycle begins and it is hard to break.

These things I am talking about is a complete runway to drive away evil. If there are any demons of darkness it is a branch of metaphysics to believe in that can develop the right patterns of renewed thinking. It goes beyond the conscious level of just being aware but to the subconscious level of creating actions to stop bad consequences. The ingenuity of the way the spirit can engineer a pathway of freedom may take some people's breath away. But if their faith has been raised to an openness of truth, it does not hesitate to embrace the new reality as it is being developed in the presence of their life.

They say there is trouble and problems around every corner. I say every little bit of positive intercession helps and I consider this a lot of a little bit.

The wonder of it all becomes a vacuum that keeps pushing out a cool breeze with refreshing thoughts to do good things that block out other thoughts that are not Godly. What is now the best way to fly the friendly skies that can be added to the sky chief disciples?

To be known

The anxiety disorder that affects mental health disorders that gets characterized with bad feelings can interfere with daily activities. They are cloned over and over in the negative state of growth thoughts from the void-noid, numb-dumb, lame-duck, sin-drome. It can cause people to hide out on the inside of themselves. That does not help the problem but the spirit man as it is received from spiritual skills starts to grow up and get all of the darkness inside of people out of them, consciously and subconsciously, thanks to God's method of therapy.

Are these new levels of skills important enough that all need to know? These skills grant the ability to break bondage from almost every ailment that mankind can face, if their heart desires to receive them, from gambling, processes of negativity, to a state of wanting to be, or on the verge of being crazy. We have been given this gift of freedom from the Lord. It is up to us to use it wisely.

It is March 15, 2018 and
I have kept in touch with what is going on.

Some would say that people's anxiety has been at an all-time low this past week. It is proof that is talking about it or sharing to the world as a huge part of dealing, healing and accepting to own what I said. It is mine. The stigma is gone when the power shifts back to you so thank you.

Now there is no more gambling with blindness, no more not seeing the future; no more foolishness because it is getting clearer every day. On the fact of being lost, we have to take the reins to lead ourselves out of individual trauma, we may walk into and upon that want to shake the foundation of our individual life is, the process is to be seen and dealt with to secure our presence and position in our life. The process of owning it and it not owning you is what is up so you won't get taken down. Work with spiritual skills as therapy.

For our future, we can outgrow the next level of trouble on the horizon to mark it before it is time and to watch it pass us by and not leave the pain on our doorstep. I talked about what was done at the RNC and the incident I had at the different rallies in Cleveland during the problems with the people and police even at the steps of the Justice Center. I tried to help people own it and understand it with the book *A Peace Offering for the Police and People*. Before it was accepted I was accosted to not bring this to the forefront. They wanted an eye for an eye and a tooth for a tooth way of resolving the issues.

Let's move on past this because the presence of the Lord still had my back and I had a soldier of the Lord with me. At the time other nations of people were there that would have not stood for the insult or any kind of ignorance that may have come my way to do me harm.

After I made the will of the Lord's presence I left to let the people defuse themselves I felt I planted the seeds to show yourself the mercy that you have been afforded to that was given to us by the Lord.

This kind of wisdom may take some adjusting of the belt so take your time this meal will last forever.

At BTHPM, we are trying to help others take charge of their life. The youth are so important in a way to make sure they have the information to fight back with light to come out of the dark side, if it comes upon them or they are approached. They need to have the wisdom to know not to gamble with what could be a curse in disguise.

It is the gambling games that may put them in a state of fire just by playing around in it or with it. It can become a bad habit if they are under age and have to think it's the only way to get ahead street gambling. It increases the odds for trouble coming their way.

We know that the abuse that hurts some people comes by way of the abuse they got and it is, in some cases, a repeat thing. Now the cycle can be broken along with the fact the new recruits that Satan wants to put to work doing his dirt can think twice before they attempt to hurt someone. The odds are against them to do the dirt and keep it under cover. This is thanks to the one fact, you can't hurt love and think you are going to get away with it. It better stop before you start the Lord knows how to make you pay for it. Now it isn't worth it at all.

This is a new kind of activation with students taking a stand.

This is a way to be a part of activists on a level of not having risky activities

This is a harmonious expression of love

I have an idea that needs to grow. It may be one of the only missing pieces that needs to go in place to increase the growth and love for community that is missing at this time. It is the harmonious expression of love throughout mankind.

We know how to help. All you have to do is ask for it. There is knowledge that awaits you to give you an understanding that you may feel bad. It will pass along with the fact you are loved. You can freeze frame anything that wants to take that away from you.

The death of young people in schools is one of the main things we can avoid. We can let them know they can stop the feeling of wanting to harm anyone including self, by giving them the ability to know they can stop.

The pain from the harm that kills rocks my soul. An example of this was when a shooter killed students in Chardon, Ohio on my birthday (Feb. 27th) in 2012. That is why I am glad to have this to offer. As far as this place, there is a shrine in Chardon. I would like to visit it from time to time. It is a kind of sacred place for me.

I stay in pain, somewhat, over the fact that whomever does harm to others is without enough love in their life, making them want to take a life to hurt. We all should have enough love that is free, but someone is starving for it so bad they kill others so that others feel the pain they have inside. What a shame and who is the blame that so much love is missing out of someone's life? If anyone is to blame, we are.

Let's all take a little of the blame and stop the devil from doing it again if we can by finding the unloved and let them know they are loved. Not trying to say a book can make up for a person's love but it can make a case of love the one you are with. If that is just you at a time when you feel no one else is there it is okay too.

If you don't know what the main reason is for the youth shooting at school, it is that youth can't protect themselves from themselves. They don't know how. Some people are vulnerable to themselves being out of control. That is why they need the additional protection that the Lord can give to keep them safe.

To help correct any deficiency in a young person there are many ways. This is just one way to outgrow the woo-woos that makes people somewhat temporarily insane. To steer the way clear of this kind of sinkhole, it requires the principles of love developed in a state of wisdom that can be received through knowledge. That is what someone gets when they read the recommended book, _The New Added Protection for the Development of Teens and Young Adults at Risk_. It gives guidelines to step aside the traps that are quickly sinking like they are in quicksand. All the black on black crime has some people with this problem. The children who have to live with it can use some intervention.

The truth of the matter is we all have to learn to flush some of a part of Satan out of us and if we can't we are flirting with dust that might create dirt devils. The youth are or may not be fully equipped to do this and need all of the help they can get at times when they are lost inside of themselves and can't get the right kind of help, meaning spiritual and perhaps they have been taunted or teased by peers.

The backfire may happen when Satan builds up an arsenal of hate that is released with hell's fury that kills.

The key to it is get the equipment to put out hell fires before they catch on to other lives. The work has been done. You can fix things. The ideas that the books have inside contain some of the best therapy in life to keep life in tune with a loving balance forever.

The last thing is we need to make sure that no child has a death wish. If there is one who has this, it needs to be fixed. Attention should come to this immediately because if not it may likely come apart on a level of others being harmed.

We must end any kind of death wish that a child or young adult has. It will help to stop the massacres in all ways in our society; schools and homes. When the fear of not dying is there, people like company (like misery does). It is time to end this kind of misery.

If the Lord challenges you to do something why not at least try? Do you need to try these books? *The New Added Protection, etc.*, a home and street safety program that add God's intervention and *Time To*

Stop Living On The Edge also _How to Live With Less and Gain More_.

Let this be like the Three Musketeers in your Life

Let's think about it. How many more are out there who are a threat to do what the latest young man did in Florida? He was lost with no love that harmed his mental ability to love others with the respect for their life enough not to harm them.

The plan is to help youth with troubles and provide them with a way out of the problems that brew or burn within and to douse the flames that cause wildfires harming others. There can be a pre-awareness plan put in place to help every student or person who thinks they are at risk to snap out of control. Read the books along with the others that are available. Contact me at tb.bthpm@gmail.com.

This is not a get well from mental illness course but a spiritual wellness treatment plan. It is a program in a book to stop the unannounced crook in someone from stealing a life. Adults: this is a great way to share home study with youth. The Lord's wisdom is priceless. I hope this is for you!!!!

This ounce of prevention is like a pound of cure

The biggest movement today is for all people to not any force push, pull or take you into the void-noid, numb-dumb, lame-duck, sin-drome. They chain you to Satan's wagon of ill repute. The train is over and done the so-called invisible one can now be seen by all mankind. It is a presence of ungodliness that may present itself in a pretty way that has man blinded with a beauty grace that can charm the pants off of you. Don't allow it because it doesn't come looking ugly at all. It sometimes comes seeming to be good but it carries a funk that sneaks up on people and gives them a kind of brain freeze that may lock them into some. That costs more than anyone should be willing to pay.

Now that you know a little more about your enemy, do you really want to hook up with them? Now that you have been read your rights God knows if you want to play a game where there is no way out. A fair exchange is going to take place. You have been had by yourself and that only means one thing: check yourself before you wreck yourself.

Now take nothing in stride that may cause you to not survive. A vice don't play with something, or someone, that doesn't play fair. A lesson from my mother.

Note: A hidden danger of the dark side of the mind that must be helped is the fixer that can save the lives of the innocent people because Satan wants them dead to not have a chance to share their gifts and furthermore, the love.

I have been teaching this for more than three decades and have been waiting for the rest of the world to catch up with my teaching. I think the time has come so be a part of the in the know we people thing. It brings wisdom to the table to have a meal and not just a meeting about a problem. It brings salvation that helps stop the danger of an unwanted action of negativity on any level, even a threat.

The pain that can create the void-noid, numb-dumb, lame-duck, sin-drome may have been let in to give some the gambling habit. It does the same thing with drug use that can come from some people getting hurt or too much joy popping. That leads to experimenting for fun. Too much of anything isn't good for you if you are not careful and there is too much fun when drugs come into it.

M-N

People take note you must know there is always room for anyone who doesn't let Satan take control over their life, believe and receive that. That goes with a crown of a halo that only God may be able to see while you are on earth.

There are signs that when people don't really think for themselves, something goes wrong. It usually happens before they know it in most cases. Then the quickness of what action that takes place slaps them in the face. Trouble of any kind that may come from being desperate about a process of growth. It could be like a plan out of not wanting to get locked out of a part of life. That requires more than you have. It seems like there is a place that has your name on it that you need to take care of or make known to the world who you are, even if it makes you out of a fool or kills you or others.

The bottom line to all of this is Satan may be in control of you and you don't know it. So the deal is to get back in control with the help you can get with spiritual skills.

Why do we get strung out into a process of growth that we shouldn't be? It is because of the gravitational pull that can get us off balance due to the earthly realm of a place that Satan has set up for people that he bets gets caught in it so he can have control over. Hey, it isn't my rule and it is what it is. That is why the other rules were made to honor thy mother and father and know who puts the rules together if they don't honor you.

When Satan said to kill the people around if your life is bad but the Lord said to know he is there and see all that the unjust will pay for their sins. The ones who are harmed that stay faithful will see the coming of the glory of the Lord.

If you don't know Satan steps in and said, sin, sin, sin! That is why you can stop hearing him through spiritual skills. Amen.

Advertisement

It is time to know that the Lord will bring his presence to a body of people when it is time to grow with love. He will stop the disturbance in the land when the prayers are right in his sight. We have seen the decrease of the killing of young black men and now that the school shootings are running a course, we want something to be done by people in charge of the land with more gun control or finding a way to make schools safe or help the people who may not be well so they don't become violent in school.

At this time, we can see by the way the reactions are taking place, the nation has a need to put plans in place to stop the madness that causes the sadness and killing.

How to close up the dark holes
inside of one's self to create light

How do we grow up? It is not running away from the real pain, the insecurities. We even go through life getting scared in life also the anxiety, the downfall, the setback, the trials, the tribulation, the misery and even the heartbreak, wasn't made for total consumption. It will raise up and slap you or a figure of speech grabs

108

you by the balls. Even with all of this that can occur in life that we are made to withstand it and then some. I'm not saying it is destiny to be confronted with this. But if you do, it is up to you to have the preparation in order to weather it.

There is no better preparation than having spiritual skills. Believe that and receive them. They are the lifeline to lots of people who have physical ailments. If it can work for them, then why can't it be used for almost all other things that relate to disconnect in life.

When I am feeling out of it in ways that may not be understood by myself and others, at times, I asked the Lord to wrap his loving arms around me and give me the comfort I am in need of to see me through the storms that I may have on the inside of me.

I ask the Lord to shelter me from myself with his loving care so I will be protected from any kind of darkness that may want to intrude on my life and to keep me safe with the comfort of his love. I thank him constantly for the gift because him alone I have faith in and always hope that he will see me through.

The Therapy

To look at the gun violence at the right view is what it is all about in the schools. We can't change everything but we can change most people's attitudes to get the help they may need this is a stepping stone.

They will give guidance to anyone who feels lost outside of themselves. They think they are not in control of their actions.

The teaching of a new way to act and respond to yourself can be challenging. If you don't resist the concept of taking in a new relationship with yourself, it becomes a cleansing stage of growth. It requires an understanding of the fact that you can become a more important person to yourself that gives a way to outgrow the past with insight of the future that can benefit the present. That is a great present to be in and want to stay a part of to add whatever two cents you can to the economy of life.

To add to it all the goal that will be set for you is not just yours to set but the spiritual presence of a gift to know in your heart: do no harm to people because they may be a reflection of the gift you are a part of to the world.

The prayers have been answered. However, the one shame of it all is it wasn't known by some who made mistakes of doing the wrong thing. All of this can be explained as order in the Christ-like universe.

My Therapy (use it too)

I have one thing to say that may sound off the beaten path. I thank people for their rejection because it gives me more reason to improve myself for me. I need to

110

get that kind of motivation to outgrow things I may
need to just because I am alive. I have gone as far as
to tell someone thank you for the rejection. It is what it
is and it shall pass.

The ABC's rendered me to a degree where I don't
need an oversight of a presence that is unhealthiness.
The roots are at hand that put life together for all
people if they want love.

How is this? To know of the before Christ; to know of
the decent of Christ; to know of the ascent of Christ;
to know of the return of Christ and to believe of the
reuniting of Christ with you.

This wisdom is not revolutionary. It is ancient and has
been used by the slaves of old European times and
Aztecs along with the native people of many lands.
The modern life has kind of left it out of the picture of
the technological age. That is why it is time to return
to the presence of the sender of healing to the people
of the world that can defend them in multiple ways
that constantly illuminate the way to bring the best
results to the lives of people.

All are welcome to experience this phenomenon of
what the love of the Lord can do that will bring a warm
feeling, and that includes you. The skills help people
accept and help to plant the seeds, cultivate, nurture
and harvest the results.

M-N

The nature of mankind will put people in the darkness all by itself because of its misdirection once it gets exposed to the void-noid, numb-dumb, lame-duck, sin-drome. That is why the love of God is there to take them out of it or help keep them from going there.

M-N

I have been preaching and teaching these spiritual skills for over 30 years.

As I close off the tap of knowledge that is running out of myself, I think it would have been nice to have had a visit from my parents in the spiritual realm of one of my dreams.

This is a part of using the good of the power of the placebo effect is the part of the human spirituality that helps in making one's self whole to the newness of growth in a new and exciting way. Sometimes the stalemate sin-drome creates an unseen enemy that may possess a kind of death wish that strikes up fear. People want company because of a kind of death wish they may be experiencing. This is why moving out of the phase of who you were supposed to be is important.

M-N

I am going to keep hopping and popping and not stopping to teach the different rules for different schools in some ways in life.

The conjunction of the spiritualism is the conductor to love. I have had a near death experience when I was about seventeen. I came back but beforehand the doctors said they couldn't do anything more for me. The Lord will have to do the rest.

It was my grandmother I didn't know, my father's mother, who said "go back and complete what the Lord has for you to do." Even though I wanted to stay there in a way.

To show how much this may be needed, if there is only one who gets something from this, it will be worth it.

M-N

There is not a religious dimension I am putting before another. I am ecumenically-minded because we all can rise together if the heart is right.

One question is, could the missing connection with the placenta come into existence when the umbilical cord is separated from a baby? If so, then can it reflect upon negativity as Satan sets up house?

The most horrific and detrimental thing I have ever done in my life three times during a period in school when I was instrumental by participating in a riot at Rawlings Jr. High School. During the process I almost seriously injured and maybe I could have killed someone by throwing them from the third floor to the first. Thank God there was someone there to stop me, an old friend of mine. There is no good thought about this story but during the mass confusion because of the rules that were set in place, I saw an opportunity to harm someone who had been harmful to others. There will never be an excuse for it. I say this to say do not allow the devil in the details of any school institution of any kind. It will weigh on you and cause sadness in your life more than you can imagine. Stay away from that kind of negativity.

What may be put in place of a bad habit is the fact of knowing you are love by the Lord if it is seen there is no one else who does. The emptiness that some may feel can be full with this process of thinking that will also remove the void-noid, numb-dumb, sin-drome, that gives an opening for sin to come in to someone's life to steal, kill or destroy it.

Respect yourself

That is one of the biggest problems youth have because they are missing it so much and if they don't get it because of it they may act out and show it to others. Just for bad consequences to come their way on and in a subliminal level they are somewhat locked into and don't think about the consequences until it slaps them in the face. Protection from self is what they need; protection from self.

Stay in front of this all life long

Anyone can have a turn at conquering negativity, in other words, Satan. I mean to shut down the three stages void-noid, numb-dumb, lame-duck, sin-drome that gives an opening to the gateway for Satan to come in. That is why to corner him you must first know his plan and that can be anything that is not good or healthy or harm or kill or make someone lame. The last is the part where people feel they can't do.

If you use his methods to defend Satan and start with shutting down the void-noid, numb-dumb, lame-duck, sin-drome. You can get caught off guard at times. But you will not get hooked to because a crack that lets Satan steal the love the Lord created for his children. Know that you will never be a lame duck that is sitting in the void-noid, numb-dumb, lame-duck, sin-drome avenues of life.

This is how you conquer the pre-arrangement of what can be done to put him out of your space in your head. So it goes no further, then whatever was written down can be tossed in the trash.

115

So we meet again in the same pathway with the Lord's love that keeps on giving forever. It will work for you time and time again. You have the Lord's guarantee to give Satan a boot to protect you. You can if you get ahead of the trouble that comes from a thought and then an action.

You have the power to unveil the enemy and know the truth that sets you free. You need to know who is on first base and whatever base they come at you from. You are the umpire that call them or it out every time it tries to go home because that is always protected by the Lord.

The system has been diagnosed with a disease that keeps people in the lame lane. They are standing around waiting for a ball to come along and knock them down. As they are set up again be knocked down again.

Well it is time to let go of the standing turmoil that puts people in a lame state of living. The unseen miracle quandaries is now known to put things right in the presence of mankind. It is a new attitude that is taking people like a healing balm. So let it be known and if you want to get the good news of this out there then I suggest you become a sky chief disciple. That way you can take it to the sky and enjoy a natural high. Everything I write about is how to stay out of the lame lanes in life, all of them.

Good idea

Spiritual proverbs present analytical behavior change on a positive level.

When you look at it you are rolling the balls, or you are letting someone else do it, until you may crack your bulb if you don't get free.

The self-list way is the best way

Next if you need to keep yourself from idling wild, it is time to think for yourself. The fact is if you don't someone or something will do it for you. The only one you would want to do that is the Lord.

As you learn to think for yourself, the one thing to be aware of is developing selfishness. I have been there and I saw others go there. At times they didn't know they were there and pointed their finger at someone who they thought had it but didn't turn their finger around. A period of time went by and they could have done some good and or they were told about themselves. These blessings are meant to be shared.

A Personal Request

If there is a child that you know that is not being loved find a way to put some love in their lives. Do this and you have done one of the greatest works that anyone could ever do in life. They are first.

Why are so many people in trouble? It is because they have the invisible sickness called not knowing enough about their spirituality. It is so common that people do not pay attention to it. They can have a fixer-upper in a matter of no time at all. When they look at how long some get lost in the wilderness once they step out of bounds into a foreign place that is one of the four death zones they are put in, void-noid, numb-dumb, lame-duck, sin-drome that can set them up for any kind of setback in life, or even set you out of life in ways like drug use, misuse of firearms. They both kill. The wakeup call is here to be not only seen or heard. It is here to show you to keep a vigil over life and for everyone.

One of Satan's biggest tools is to make sure one feels lonely, left out, not worthy of friendship, isolated, even though they may not be on that level. Once he gets his wedge in place it can seem like that. If a person starts to believe it, it will slowly take place or the withdrawal affect will bring someone down.

That is why the compass has to be turned around by the skills of spirituality to fix the problems on whatever level it is on, whether not good, bad or ugly. The new attitude can come about with the quickness. Thanks to God's plan of action that keeps people going strong.

This book causes people to really think and not do something stupid. It gives them a new connection with themselves. It is a book that helps to bring out the best in someone. There are so many good things that can be learned from this book. I can only say to experience it is to know of a better part of you that you may have been missing.

This book can help teach someone how to have a giving and loving spirit. That is one of the best things in the world to have that money can't buy. It can also be a gift that keeps on giving throughout a lifetime and maybe beyond.

To take a trip on a self-taught spiritual quest to enhance the love that a person has. It can be one of the greatest odysseys a person may want to experience. don't forget about the additional protection of one's self with God's intervention to enhance the growth of day to day living and give a person an added edge of goodness in life. Get to know this book and you may get to know yourself better than you do now.

It is time to stop the enemies to the state that work for the state.

What gets on my nerve is when someone wants you to want or need them so badly that they are haters who want to take you out of your comfort zone to see if you sweat. Now what is wrong with them? They are so full of themselves and they forget to clean their butts because it stinks even if no one else can smell it but them. If I do not have enough to do with keeping myself in order as I was growing up.

To develop the consequences of the reality of being delivered from the sin of not knowing what has, know what could or what will affect your life is a key to keeping out in front of the problems that take people down in life and/or try to keep them down if not putting them in a worse place.

Therefore, let the troubles and problems and if need be the people, places and things see the dust that you leave behind, as a smokescreen to blind everything from seeing you again.

If you just acknowledge spiritual skills are a part of the grace the Lord gives us, it is a protector at the least. It is a new phase of growth. I am working on something else for you to get to know later and it is the keep the blood blue presence of thinking that won't be out before November 2018 I hope you will look forward to receiving it.

This is another stay on the right track and weather the storm I have been there and done that. An endeavor was started on five years before this but will not be ready for you until later this year. The keep your bliss club. It is to not let your circumstances of bad times and a hard coming out of an abuse or any kind of trauma that you have experienced. Defeat the love you have inside of you that can do you wrong or cause you to do yourself wrong by doing someone else wrong.

I have been in the kingdom building business of helping people to get to their salvation. At this time, I may have overrun the runway. I am trying to not come to a conclusion that people can be afraid of my writings or are they can be afraid of what it can teach them about themselves. Who wants to learn about their personal gifts the Lord has for them and how the Lord wants them to receive it?

To understand David and the fact that as king he was the largest and tallest man who ruled the country. He was, in the people's eyes, supposed to fight Goliath. To understand this gives a great presence of knowledge.

What is the main reason Satan tries to take the Lord's people to keep us off balance? He wants to distract us from the Lord's work we all need to be doing.

Why do youth kill? They are living in so much darkness and blindness and fail to see, know and feel real love. They see others around them having a good time in ways that haunt them and give them daytime nightmares. This can cause them pain. They feel compelled to share if they have no understanding of crises intervention.

The Lord died for you on the cross and his pain cannot be compared you have nothing missing or broken because of it and you can weather any storm except for hell. Always remember that come on line every time there is a problem that we cannot handle. That is so cool to have a God-like computer at work for you all the time 24/7. Learn to let new news sink in because you let it get old and it should never.

The worse thing society has done to the youth is bury some of them before they are helped to get grounded. Now they have no need to be afraid any longer to life because of these kinds of messages and more.

That is what the real reason is afraid to live and harm others. Did we make it where some people feel that way? If so, how do we change it? With love and additional wisdom. How to get that way on a moral level and also a natural accord along with the upbringing if one parent has a problem it can split the possession of a life in two, leaving an opening for the void-noid, numb-dumb, lame-duck, sin-drome. It is like idle land that Satan wants to set up strife in to do his kind of dastardly deeds to harm the people God loves. It is one of Satan's hopes and dreams. He gets them, noting he also wishes for you to be his also. Do not get caught up in his hype that leads you to the wrong permanent home sight.

The holiness of biblical wisdom

To the acknowledgment of the people who have displayed their focus on change, who took to the streets and marched, I am with you. To the multitudes that went to Washington, DC., I am with you 110%. It is hoped that more of the gun laws change daily.

What can come next is the God laws of mankind that got lost in the adjustment of growth in a lot of people. They need a revival to make known to have the self-control or to entrust it to the Lord's laws. They has to be set up to be set in motion in people who may have the possibility to fail the self-governing system of self-control. It is as simple as that. No one is perfect and some have more self-control than others. I was one for whatever reason I had.

I had it doesn't give me an excuse to do the wrong thing anymore. I know I don't want the pain in someone's life or to have to face the consequences. That is why people change and adopt God's laws that can protect us as humans from ourselves if need be. All I can say about them is Amen and Hallelujah because they really work.

I would like you to know I didn't get permission to use anyone's name. I hope you forgive me for any mistakes you find in this book. If you find one or some it only means you are better than me in some ways. I will feel good about that as strange as that may sound. I would like you to be better and do better than me. I also didn't have anyone as I always do beside myself help me with the education but the same people I have had for years with one new person.

It is a blessing to allow Dr. God to manifest the blessings of his love to cure any sickness of any kind. I hope when someone knows of this happening to them they testify and spread the love as they receive it.

These live the mighty of life

There is no tripping planned on this level of learning. We can go on a field trip about things in life that at times we may wish we didn't.

This is not that kind. If there is a problem in life with people it creates some kind of pain. Now at the most we can do is find a way to help get relief and if there is no relief in sight or someone thinks it can't be relieved found it can and will cause them to lose it or crack their bulb, snap and go crazy.

This kind of pain that acts like Carbon Monoxide poisoning that affects the spirit and numbs it to deaden it. It has a detector, the spiritual skills detector reflector. It senses the problems because of the increase the presence of love.

This is how it gets done

God's love grows daily and some people are not aware of that. But you are now being made aware so use it to keep it moving to help stop pain that causes traffic jams in the pathway to heaven. Satan wants to put a stop to the highway to heaven. You know what is said now when you are in the school of learning how to be Christ-like, if the study is testing the teacher doesn't say anything. But it is time to start time to stop.

In between the process of getting in your Sunday school help with every test is theirs. So now are you at Sunday school and don't know it? The reason I say this is every day is a Sunday school moment and it never stops. Getting to the next level past the pain is the gain to look into the future. See how you can increase the Sunday sunny days that leads to the Sunday moments for others in the country and the world.

Are you going to live the best commitment speech there ever was that wasn't spoken about but shows in the days to come that made a better life for all people? Whatever commitment speech the Lord gives you to live, live it.

I would hope that this new book to stop people from killing at all schools can be a catalyst to help show the young how to get the country back in God's grace.

As it seems sometimes we all have to make a last ditch effort to receive a reward. This can be one of mine.

I tell myself how much I have given back to the people I know I had it to give by the grace that was shown to me by the Lord. I have depended on the Lord to give me the guidance and bless me enough to have a family and grandchildren that I will be able to think of them all as being proud of me.

The dreams that came to me of my mother and others are my highlights also. They keep me in check.

The headline is how to think your way out
of trouble be for it come your way!

The treat others as you want to be treated pledge
or the sustaining your life pledge

I have honestly accepted the book as a way to combat my mental anguish and to learn from it. I am in charge of my emotions. I am also not going to let my blessings in life be destroyed from myself losing control because of anyone or thing that I may harm another with the exception of protecting me or my family.

It is with great honor that I am taking in not only learning how to protect myself from myself but to share it with others. I am committed to remain a humanitarian to the day I die and then some.

I sign this pledge with love to bring out the best in me for all to see. I commit to do no harm to another as a child of God.

I can't say I have learned as much as I would like to know from the presence in my lifetime. One stand out that leads me to believe in the fact that peace creates the only true way to democracy throughout the world. This gives me strength to know that my ideas are fundamentally based of the same thing, even if it leads me to see if I am able to show a nation of people how to prevent or stop war in the name of Jesus.

If I see a way into the places in the world that need to help themselves out of their dilemma, am I responsible to give them the right way to take themselves out of a dilemma? Of course! Therefore, I can say if I can get in to show them I can do the duty it is not up to me to get me in but to get the message in.

I will need help to do this. The only way I feel it can be done is by the will of the Lord that I may be used to bring this forth. Do I have the will? Let's see, I know there are hedges and walls that surrounds communities and nations. Therefore, it is the visible that will have to be defeated by the invisible that has the power to appear or give a command that the Lord gives you to make it happen even if you are not there.

I have two examples. One the Ronald Reagan saying "Gorbichov, take down that wall," or the walls of Jericho that came down. Let's look at a nursery rhyme, Humpty Dumpty. If the leader on a place has the wrong man-child attitude then they are more than likely a towerist. If someone knows how to handle them in the right way, they can take the wall down for their people or they will play on it so much it will cause them to fall off of it and crack their bulb.

They will give the people they are ruling over to become free. There are so many ways to skin a cat but the best way if they don't come down out of the tower is to know the Lord will bring them down.

When people are denied human rights, you must present them with the facts of knowing spiritual wisdom that gives them the indication of one fact that you are aware and awaken to. The fact is, you are not blind to them wanting to misguide you to become better than you thought you ever could be with this different vision of growth.

To take it to another level of belief, the Lord is not fake. Now who is spreading the fakeness around in any way they can, Satan, he is the author of being fake. He even wants you to think the Lord is fake.

Some people believe you from the rights you are
entitled to as a human, right defender.

People get your sainthood to that, who are
supposedly wise. Thank God I can do it.
In the spirit of his anointing that he is you so that you
can receive your deliverance.

The towerist that stay as they are, who do not want to
receive change are now to be known as toiletry
people, that wants to remain cursed.

One of some of the youth hardest tasks is to not make
it harder to respect their partner if they cannot get
away from them.

Stop being the oo-goos people have to stop thinking
they know about that crap. When people think they
are so important they forget about others they are full
of that, which is only a substitute for doo-doo.

The sainthood status in your life by going back to
retrieve the steps of freedom, etc. the abuse etc., the
messages etc. so on so forth that will end in you
having a place to start.

If you develop a cloak of wisdom it makes you a
hooded saint disciple. That is one who has a power
given to them by the Lord. They will know how, why
and where to use it.

Hooded Sainthood Disciples

Sainthood disciples can have two sets of wings, one to fly and the other as spares to help you keep your faith. To know these things that come in the wisdom of the Lord with an understanding how to perform the obligation that belong to them, gives you the self-respecting honor of the pledge of a gift to be presented to the world.

We have come to a fork in the road to give us the truth about ourselves. We have been getting fooled by fake news in life, but it is fake faith that we have on a level of self-belief. We have become reluctant to face what is being done.

The fake faith has us believing in people who give us what we think we need to believe in, instead of what we know to be true. It is a fantasy life we want to be a part of that is now real also.

The good thing is, this is real news instead of fake news that we have been relying on in the blind side of fake faith we have in part of the people in America. To get down to the real news once again, there has been more than enough trash and dirt tossed on me. It made me no different than others, until I woke up.

The one thing that we all have is common is we have the power to deliver ourselves from demon spirits that try to destroy us and captivate us in a fake style of life. With the new presence of wisdom we can recognize, revive, and penalize the enemy by dismissing them.

This is your note to self

The Lord is still raising people up from the dead. He is the only one that can do this. That is included in the history of life on earth, believe it to receive it. If you have the wrong faith, it is death. Faith without works is also death.

To help you understand the political climate, the new book by Madilyn Albright can give you a step up or step down into serenity. It can give you a helpmate to the vision that needs to be received in 2025.

The people of the USA have fervent prayers to the opposition of the discombobulation of the negative prospect of the fake news that was indicated by more than one country. It may have caused a shift in the presidential election. We no longer have to let ourselves be subject to their rhetoric thinking. Fool us once shame on you, but not anymore thanks to our foresight that will stop the un-purposeful garble. If anyone still wants to be prejudice in life, be prejudice of untruth.

Big news

The new level of heroism that trumps all other isms is yours to receive to add blessings to your deliverance.

Now I come to my fork in the road. I know it seems like the people who love the Lord the most should be the ones running the world. I think it has been towerists running the world. Now the Lord sent his team of disciples out to declare to the world his good news. Now it is time for a new level of disciples to start running the world with the presence of actions like never before. It will be shown by the blessings that we keep in our midst to manifest more.

The fact of being thankful alone will and can generate an energy that can supply the world over and over again. If we the new disciples show the way to this, the Lord will do the rest.

The great thing about the book, *Fixing What's Broke in America by Stopping Towerism* is, it can show people, men mostly, how to get to a place where they can stop trying to be one the world's greatest chauvinists, that causes them to not display sensitivity to women and want to treat them like a piece of cattle and use them unequally and should not be.

It is truly time for people to take back the future of our history. Do not let Satan dictate it like he has been in parts of our past.

This can be done more so after the development of becoming a sky chief disciple. Then, if you would like, get your sainthood and grow it along with your discipleship. It all is a way of life that keeps getting better with hooded saint discipleship, which this book will help you achieve.

In every neighborhood in the world there should be some of the workings of this process. This thinking can be like developing a state of sainthood thinking by way of someone's actions that moves them up in kingdom building to fulfill the cause of structure with the addition of learning. The word hood is a covering and there is not enough of them in the world. The Lord chose to recruit more in this fashion. Now, let the power of the Lord come in. Amen and Hallelujah!

Wake up to this

This was created to un-complicate the doctrine of the Lord to know of His truth to be a part of His living will, while doing His will. I had to ask the Lord "what am I doing?" He said, "Write out a part of my real so others can know it also." Now to do what I do it almost makes me feel like I am blind and do not want to see anything other than the next thing the Lord would have me write.

Binding up the wounds to do all of this we need to stop towerism by growing to get the job done to tame the sovereignty of man. This is the cleansing of our society from the other kind of violence.

A personal experience I had

I have a mission to un-taint a level of people who have toxic souls that are not free to love. In this new book I come to recognize that when I had an episode of wanting to commit harm to myself it was. I read a book that the towerist was using to get rich and I did something it said to not do. I thought it would keep me poor for it, what a foolish person I was. I will never be foolish over what is said in a book. I wanted to hurt myself because I could not be a towerist.

The moral to this process of thinking is, I became toxic with Satan's sickness that caused my eternal soul to need a transplant of spirituality to become detoxified of the bondage Satan had me under. His trickery blinded me from reality and set me in a dark place where I could not see the forest for the trees.

This is the perception he puts on anyone in any way he can, every chance he gets, to cause people to end their lives because of the inner pain and pressure of torment they find themselves under. Thank God I went through the pain and pressure but through the seeds of spiritual endowment I was able to weather the storm. Anyone who knows this truth can weather storms. They must know God's Son roof can open a way up into the clouds to get them out of the tunnel where there seems to only be darkness that comes before them. Amen!

Spiritual skills create detoxification from the poison that is feeds into the system constantly as it creates filters so that a human spirit can stay well and healthy.

My numbers may not be correct but April 12, 1865, ended a certain part of reality even though it started in 1840. This was the beginning of a coming back together as a country, the city of hope better known as Cleveland in my perception of thinking is the place that the hearts of many of mankind have developed from. Now we can begin the steps of coming back together as Americans starting in Ohio with a new kind of spiritual revolution. This may be the only way to do this.

We cannot put a dollar amount on a life-saving treatment or process of rescue. If we do, do we count our life the same way? Therefore, do all you can at this time so more can live from what we give that amounts to love without a loss. We can always think up!!

I really want to meet the world, it is a dilemma I feel I have born to show, a part of it as a pathway to an eternal heaven. I can help to do this with the world wide ministry I am founding by using more than the forty books I have authored. One such book helps people to receive their personal gift from the Lord to bless others *All Peoples Handbook*.

The other books will help stop people from killings at all schools plus put the country back in good grace with the Lord. There are three books that help to develop the new discipleship levels the country is in need of because of the towerist that have been running the country and a part of the world.

I tell myself I have enough to give back to the people and the sky is the limit. This letter is to myself to remind me of the mission the Lord has charged to my heart I hope to share with others.

This will give information basically to teach people how to freeze frame bad things from happening in their life to be able to check the picture before it is taken. So if need be refocus the picture so it will be beautiful, not ugly just in case you are on a 0 to 60 in a split second type of situation from your reaction time that has not been readjusted in a way that keeps your flash frame in life on a positive level. That way you come out of a situation not having regrets you do not have to think of the same things over and over again, such as if I could take back that minute or second, or if I could take back what I've done because you have allowed your skills to be developed, meaning **being aware consciously and knowledgeably** (BACK). This stops the dead conscience syndrome from attacking you.

To invent a space matter message to check the level of space matter to see if there is an increase when someone is feeling bad or down or depressed that can indicate the weight of the space has increased and/or taken up more space, would mean the devil is in the details of the area that overloads the place and takes from the peace of real estate of thought by adding more weight that is unhealthy. In return, it makes it uncomfortable and that equals sadness, madness, etc. that leads to creating a hell fire burden.

Unfortunately, the only way it seems you can get an invention like this is you invent it in your mind. At the same time, if we take some of the time and energy and resources that we spend on the race for space and put it to use on a project like this, it may prove to be a better pay off than the one that goes to space. I think of it like this if you go to heaven you get the treat of seeing the milky way whenever you feel like it.

Stopping a part of fear

Putting in spiritual food is like adding the right antibodies to kill the toxic desires that will clean up the space in order to stop the crowing of the mind, heart and spirit.

Crowing of the mind can be defined as a black crow that sits around like a vulture. The crow doesn't want the dead, it wants to pick with a human that causes agitation and disturbance that lurks in a dark place that makes them want to display their peace, crowing. It is like subconsciously wanting to find an existed outside of one's self. It becomes frightening when someone wants to take others with them and at the same time not want to harm others. Now that isn't an excuse but if it has some truth to it, it may be a process of fixing a part of the love dimension we can work on.

This is when the Bengal tiger's expression comes in to deny the crowing of anyone's level of awareness. It confuses the love that was born to be known that resides there in the first place.

How many people are the good shepherds in desire that support the team effort to make things right with Bound to Heaven Publishing/Ministries?

One of the questions I have is, does having spiritual skills make you a spiritualist? Or are you just spiritually endowed? But any way if you are spiritual minded it's a great chance you won't be saintly blinded. Oh well, I guess it doesn't matter whether you have the title of being a spiritualist or not!

Can we take care of business together or is this a kind of monopoly that only a certain class of people have a right to?

Now after all this time you have been around can we finally get some help out here for the ungodly spirited people who need it? They have a chance at a degree also, that the government cannot add to it unless it changes. I am sure the people of our nation will approve upon it once it is known!

Help Cure Sin-fluenza

Sin-fluenza is like a blinding force, like someone who is without wisdom would like to believe they can commit a crime and get away with it but they need a wakeup call from it. Now deso someone call a crime a state of perception in the un-fluenza that caused me to label, or I didn't have enough of what I needed to be my defense?

Do you display sin-fluenza? If so then spiritual-fluenza means what? Again, spiritual-fluenza is not having what you need or is it having what you need?

Anti-sin-fluenza can be what spiritual skills create!

If you fake the funk and say I have no power to do a thing with what you have the furry will come back to hunt you in life because I only represent who sent me! Simple as that!

Spiritual sanitizing state of mind that has a detoxification of sin that can be fixed with the skills! Will you help? Try it to see if it can work! It will cost less than a hell sentence for some people to have to pay for? The skill creates a reduction in sin microorganisms that are of public health importance, skill disinfecting, power have a place to be reckoned with to establish and counter in as a reliable source.

The source is consistently in good quality and is a performance able to be trusted, dependable and well-founded authentic by of valid genuinely of a sound true. That has a trustworthy qualities that can be reliable and very supporting to someone in any state of crises!

This is an extra added measure of love;
This can be a definition of spiritual skills

The detoxification of a physiological or medicinal removal of a toxic substance from a living organism including the human body. Which is mainly carried out by the liver, if not it's of a different presence, but is not of a human matter. This is a present of a spirit kind. That the present of it made for only un-lawful purpose any we can disclaim any and all of it!

The removal of all harmful substances, such as poison and toxic waste by any means necessary we can achieve. So can we consider this placement that is a kind of detoxification or extra cleansing natural resource center to turn to if it has not been tried by some? That may have the best side effects ingredients money can't buy. That's less costly and the fact it doesn't affect someone's diet and you can never have an over dosage of it.

We need to have a kind of rating and a reviewing about this as if it was a consumer product that is given away by the government to the people to make it more safe from the harmful thing in life, no matter what their statement is. This will make and increase happiness in our nation!

If we can defend an age old century process of growth in a new standard of non-plagiarism should it be our mission to do so? We can use the laws of God to fix what can't be seen originally, even though it is plagiarized to sustain people to an old light made new, education can support the result with the knowledge and skills

Beginning placement

We must equip ourselves with spiritual skills, by any means necessary. If we don't we are the ones who have the appropriation of wrongful expressions. Now who do we have to lean on better than the will of the Lord? If we are our own representation of his original work we should know how to use his detector/checker to fix or use when we get broken.

It should be like having a big green button in front of us at all times to push, sit back and without attribution create a connection with submission to academic working of spiritual guidance to a place for spiritual health care. Amen!

To fix and understand: this can be one of the biggest weapons to fight a collision we might create ourselves. It probably can help people on all levels of life out of poverty of any kind. It can become a part of our national security force to help bring about a new kind of justice and freedom that people have been waiting on for so long!

Let's make it happen! In the name of the Lord! Now how is this to add to the saying I am proud to be an American!

The keys in this wisdom are endless

The analogy creates a reality that brings people closer together. It shows them how much we are alike. It helps to end the division of a level of prejudice and brings people together in new ways that may have been lost to the common state and in common mind set-up.

If we use the healing power of spiritual skills we can head off and stop some of the spiritual warfare Satan has planned for the country in the year 2025. We will also be heading off man-made disasters that take place on a level of a kind of civil war.

The ugliest show of this kind of turmoil was during the first civil war. It got so bad they had to have priests/clergymen come in the place of devastation after the death of so many soldiers. They put an exorcist on home and land where soldiers died because their spirits were not willing to move on, and it was sickening.

I know of this because I witnessed a tormented spirit that hung on to make hell steal as they did before they died! To shun the unnatural present of a demon is a way to show the power of the Lord that works in you.

There are always dysfunctional people who feel they have been done wrong and in lots of cases they have done themselves wrong and do not want to face it. But they get by even if they go through the embarrassment of losing everything. But for some their pride can eat them alive and the pain of them making themselves out of a fool, causes them to snap and want to share the pain. Does this make them shallow in life? They may deal with the superficial too much and not show up to pain and challenge it as an adult and young adult. It is time for a crash course for you need one regarding how to get it, just remember the laws of average gives people one or more in life and the Lord will see you through it.

The Lord will see you through it!!

It is time to come out of the lump of poop! Now has the generation weakened or have we lost out on having spiritual skills available to give you a spiritual guide? What do I need? I believe the trauma that the people of the slavery days was much more than the trauma in today's use. But what keep them strong the faith and belief of old spiritual song that made them strong.

Jewish people who faced the Holocaust had music that kept them strong, but the words that don't create worship and hope are not alive as in previous times. The words of today are kill, destroy, hate, disrespect and it has, of course, a lot of loss of morals. The words need to create love. Amen and Hallelujah

Okay

This is a part of God's analytics to use his algorithm for the data that needs to be placed in our spiritual reality of love to share with self and others. We can share in the security of understanding the growth patterns of spirituality as one with the Body of Christ.

There is a bottom to the void-noid numb-dumb lame-duck sin-drome. It is the deep dark cavern that houses death. Satan wants you to enter so do not oblige him and go there.

The presence of positive thinking

Within the parable that obliges us to use the placebo affect is mysterious, pervasive and clinically important. Here we discuss what it is and theories as to how the placebo affect works. If you think this is a fake treatment, let your heart make you feel and take a chance you won't regret within your faith and to succeed.

What made my eyes open

I must have been about 4 years old, at a time when it was one of the home going trips to my grandparents farm in Mississippi. The thing that brought me to an awakening was watching them work hard at getting a bull to market. The ring in its nose had so much blood coming out of the bull's face it unnerved me and created a reaction in my life on how much it put up a fight just so no one could get it into the truck for transport to slaughter. The bull had never been in a truck. It fought with every ounce of its strength to not go as if it knew it was going to the slaughter house. I think it may have seen others take that trip and never saw them again. Now it scared me to almost messing on myself. I looked into its eyes and it gave me the presence of it is worth the fight to the end for your life. Never give up without a fight. I guess subconsciously the bull instilled the fight in me even as I laid near death at one time in my life and when I thought I was going to harm myself to fight to keep the light lit in you as long as you can.

At the time all of the fighting was going on it never gave me an ounce of fear that the bull would harm me. My grandfather who owned the bull along with other relatives were all there to help. The more I think about it I wish I could have helped the bull.

The invisible bandages can work

Binding up the wounds is what people try to do but we need to bind up the wounds with love and identify them with respect. This is the best way to fix them. Trying to buy or pay yourself out of a wound someone has is not the right thing to do. Don't do it. To stay free of a handicap that some people are wearing is what you need to be doing and not contributing to.

When you are tuning into the nitty-gritty things do not get stripped or teased. On another level, I had not realized I had somewhat overshot the runway but don't you do the same. This work amounts to making things better for you and yours. Do not let this pass you by.

The Lord has heard the cries and prayers. He has felt the compassion for the pain that came from the missing loved ones who had been moved from people's presence. There is no complete end to all ends that people may see. God wants you to know this life is a part of a short term basis of reality.

This is a gift of a portal to a better state of growth with a new kind of dimension of love. Enter into a plan with the Lord to engage and ease your heart and mind. It will give to all of the movements on the land of America to go forth throughout the world as a bird in flight with an olive branch. It could take the "Youth Movement" for the school killings, the "Me Too Movement," the "Black Lives Matter Movement," and the rest of them to get you to see and know what you are part of as we all stand together.

Another tune

This can become one of the greatest ways to break out of the fortnight magnetization to get with a real level of growth that lasts for an eternity living as a real knight beats any kind of fortnight that is only a game. Nothing is wrong with fun but if it gets to be obsessive it too is a health risk and no gambling allowed with health factors.

This may be an alternative to gaming with the see us make it happen game that takes on projects and fixes them in the land we live in. The App is being put together that has a real time reality presence of a principle to help the needy become wiser and the greedy stop being that way.

Restart and reuse the energy that has become wasted in order to not want to replenish the energy in a negative way, you can find joy in a new dimension of spending your time at things worthwhile.

Towerism makes scandalism

What does this mean? It means the people that are trapped in towers feel as if they have to comply to their own kind, that gives them an edge over other people. The tragedy of it all is the country has been ruined and downgraded and made to look foolish because of the latest exposure from the new president Trump. It is trumping others to abandon the ship. He is a new level of towerist that came in as a foreigner and doing damage but at the same time draining the swamp. He acts as if he is the pied piper to run the rat-finking people out of town that is a part of "government".

We must identify the scandalous people who have really been running the country. Unfortunately its reflection gives me an unsettling feeling in my thinking that a television show has implemented the procedures of satisfying one's self for the good of the country to end the beginning of public scandals.

It seems as if there are enough people bailing out that makes it a kind of sacrifice. They know destruction and chaos has become a part of the "regular agenda".

Where do the people of America go from here? We move forward with the knowledge and wisdom that creates the power to create the rebirth of our nation to be even better than ever. Now that the scab has been ripped off it has uncovered the cesspool of indignity that was on a level of faking people out and faking the fact that the government was running the government. All the time it was the towerists that were running a part of the government that needs to be eliminated.

May this be the rock that has fallen into the pond of life that creates the ripples that goes beyond the seas and oceans so that the rest of the world can be a part of this cool breeze of happiness that comes with revealing the truth that the Lord sees to release his joy upon.

Starting again and turning the tide

To help curve the enthusiasm to becoming a gaming junky, which has serious consequences to it, you need to invest as much time into another kind of game. This game may not be one you like or ever played before. It may take you out of your way in some ways and it may make you feel like you have taken a step into history. It is the game of horseshoes the brick and mortar game compared to high tech state of modernization.

What does it offer compared to the neuronistic game? If there is no definition for "neuronistic," it has been determined that between the void-noid darkness that leaves someone open for a possible predator to enter to make someone's life seemingly lame to a degree they do not know how to duck out of the way when something wrong is headed toward them. It is a game that challenges foremost. All who play on a physical earthly level that stabilizes the material world, not like trying to stabilize the abstract world. To be honest, that has a way of taking people into a dark side of growth that can open them up to harm, by the control it takes from someone over themselves!

If I have to explain it you, you may never get it because it forces people to create a loss in life. This may include bad habits that are hard to break, which can break the spirit of some people. That is why I recommend that if you are going to try some of the abstract games that you add another level of participation to your life. The kind that makes horse sense.

It is a bigger gamble to not get some kind of insurance when the casualties are having such a hard time getting back on track to outgrow and expand their life! The next level of insurance is to become some kind of naturalist that takes care of animals and/or supports a place to help the needy. If you invest your time on a 50/50 basis it will help you be productive with our time and have days filled with kingdom building activities.

This is the pre-planned insurance for those who may fall under the ungodly spell of gambling part of their life away on a gaming level of haziness, laziness, non-caring, non-responsible or any other process that comes from the wrong side of a bad habit. It adds an "ism" to someone's system and puts them in a stalemate for the right kind of progress they need to have going on in their lives.

Sinobolic - someone who is on a sin-diet of not sinning.

I have outlived some the best people you would want to know. Let me do what is good in my life so all would share off of it. Allow this to remember me by.

It says what it means and it is as simple as that.

Bad news that was fake news
Do we have a common country?

In America 40 million people live in some kind of poverty.

Where is the faith-based money if the government has any of that? Can we put a fund in place of $40 million to help change it?

Come join the spiritual wellness institution center for a new government.

Today, can I say this is a part of redefining or defending a part of reality that has been left in the shadow of life? That is a question only we can answer individually. I will move forward with it in hopes some may catch up with me and pass me by.

Empirical – informative candid thoughts from someone who knows about smart pens and dyslexia for students.

Try to help even if it is not accepted

This gives the birth of the center for spiritual wellness control to deal with the space invader problems that have always been present. For the record, this is what the $13 billion should have been put in. it would have done more good than the atta boy toy, a towerist trying to put together spiritual wellness control.

It is my position to let the country know it needs to expand the CDC and or develop a new department to handle the next level of sickness that comes from the earthly process of entering the world through its ungodly atmosphere.

I went as far as to let the CDC know that it could be a spiritual desire of a foreign kind that causes the youth to commit suicide in Stark County, Ohio, as well as other areas. I think they just went up to investigate as a kind of witch hunt to take a kind of unofficial vacation. If you wanted to learn something you would not have left any stone unturned even if it came from

the left field that was left out of the equation; that was
me.

Come open up a can of problems for the country that
adds to the loss Hillary had of the presidency. All that
men have meant God can do some good out of it. The
change was needed that has caused that may never
had come without it. That is the hard pill to swallow.

This is the healing that the USA needs. If we believe
in the Lord as we should, we would not think of things
such as a space odyssey device that cannot work.
We are not intelligent enough to make it work and we
fail to realize our limitations. We still want to create
things to so-called protect ourselves that is somewhat
unrealistic. I hope you see where we need to go and
where we need to stop going.

Taking it to a different kind of level

Learn as David did once he became the most
powerful person in Israel to leverage the things
around him and bring an understanding to all others.
It helped to save the world at one time and it can, if
you let it, move you and your life in ways that will help
save a part of the world again. To understand this
better you need to read the following:

2 Samuel 4:10-11;
John 13:14;
Luke 5:10, 13, 18; and

John 9:7-8.

This is for the towerists to understand better how to use, and humble themselves with, their power. If Jesus washed the disciples' feet and he was willing to wash your sins free from you and take off the chains that bind people up to set them free, what should you be willing to do for humanity?

Create a kind of fitness service to strengthen the heart with accessories that come together within the spirit and consciousness as a treatment flows through you as a kind of mediocrity treadmill that is indefinitely there until it massively improves the positive ways of someone's life.

The new creation of the project that deals with the center for spiritual wellness control will be a place that can also decrease the need for mental facilitation for some people, along with incarceration. If we cure the ailment of spiritual illnesses it will also contribute to stopping the madness that creates the sadness because of physical, verbal and sexual abuse, and violence.

What other people of the world are creating that is a negative ingredient of growth is the fact that their sin nature is not as negative as someone else's sin nature.

The fact of the matter remains that if it is wrong it is wrong. When people try to escalate their counterparts wrong to a certain measure to make them look not so wrong. they are basically deceiving themselves and trying to deceive others to make themselves a knight in shining armor, which is all counterfeit anyway.

We have to accept the fact that in the political arena this is the fight to create a perpendicular process of "I am not the one to be blamed for the process that developed the maladjusted process that developed sin that fell upon a multitude of others."

What can we do? Accept the truth that you cannot fool everyone all the time and you can never fool God, no matter how you twist and turn your own reality that you are there alone, and no one has to agree with you. People who are angry who are portraying themselves in another light and others who disagree with their portrayal of themselves have twisted their own reality. End this foolishness because it is a part of towerism.

There is $120 million that the government has allocated for cyber-security. They have not used any of the money as of the time of this writing.

Feet dragging needs to stop

If we take a look around we can find lots to do with our time that is worthwhile.

The process of what I am thinking about is cyber-space intruders in the dimension of computerized technology. The cyber-space intruders are in the spiritual realm of reality and are not identified with as a mechanism of any kind. They are a complete invisible identity that we can do something about.

Once we stop that level of cyber-space intrusion we can hopefully gain better ground with stopping other cyber-space intrusion. In other words, using spiritual skills to defeat the satanic powers of darkness that we are blinded to with our eyes but not blind to our subject of what they can do to cause pain and harm.

Because of all the problems I experienced, I have lived on the edge but you do not have to.

Enough killing at schools. This is a prescription to throw away the other kind of misguided perception that shows the way for anyone to stop the killing at any level of school before they do it.

To get lost in the right part of yourself is what will start to take place in some people's lives that can keep bringing the best out of them.

A good read is "A Great Road" by Simon Schama.

M-N
for Me

It is nice to be able to get up in the morning and look across the world and see what I am doing that is adding to more peace in the world.

M-N
Foggy

They say that some people think they are too smart to read. Most of them are really too dumb to think very much.

The parametric wisdom of the Holy Spirit which has to be known is that the Lord is in all people. It gives the presence of the instruction or improvement of a person, morally or intellectually. It uplifts the training/tutelage and makes the way to get the translations more of a joy and an edification from the books I have written. It helps people to allow the intercessor to take control and protect their thinking/actions, permeates and spreads throughout a filter of cleaning oneself of ungodliness. It diffuses thoughts in the membrane that are not healthy to create a lovely way to go in an osmosis that can only be developed through synonyms/antonyms that have been taught from the companies of love.

The books have a presence that helps detoxify people of sin. Once this is done, the individuals will not have the use for any type of gun. There is more than one way to help solve a problem, true enough to help stop the bump stock process of an automatic weapon is a great thing to do.

The sad fact is someone who is determined to get their hands on a gun to cause harm may not be stopped in time. We can help fix this problem that some consider a mental illness that personally I think may be somewhat just half of the problem, if that much, even though people like or enjoy or feel safe by putting labels on every damn thing it is unfortunate they sometimes label things wrong, excuse my expression.

Refocusing some of the energies that we do may bring us to a new and better conclusion of not only dealing with a problem, but fixing it. If we fix some of the problems dealing with sin part of the problems dealing with mental illnesses will dissipate. It is a fact that has been proven throughout history. It is the way the Lord works believe it to receive it, I can witness to it. I've been there and He has done that in my life time and time again. You may say this is in conjunction to your belief, faith, and studying to be approved of changing ones circumstances.

This is a way to dissipate sin nature that was brought or came into someone's life at birth, but did not affect everyone in the same way. Some had it worse than others. There is no explanation for this, but some sin nature increases because of the environment some people come up in and around them. The good part of it is anyone can get free from it.

The strange thing is when you learn the wisdom of the Lord, it has a fixer upper set of rules that automatically kick starts a regiment that helps free people from themselves. Some people get locked up inside of themselves and cannot find their way out.

The hazy part is they think they are protecting themselves and are not. So the wisdom of the Lord if taught the right way can show them a way out. Now, the psychological experts can do this somewhat also, but I think the Lord has a better chance of getting it done in a way that last forever and it's not as costly or time consuming. In other words, it can be a better all-around therapy experience.

There are different levels of treatment: one for self, one to help while others are treated by someone abusing them so that it can stop, also the process of getting along with police officers, which may be included. The books generate love and target versions who do not know the God kindness that He wants to share with them.

This is one of the most crucial times some parents are facing as well as their offspring or child they are guardian over.

Overview to look into

The state of a child wilding out is enormous pressure of an intenseness that can leave some parents/guardians emotionally drained. That is why I am stating you may save some time and energy also and emotions or the big feeling of having to watch what is considered your love investment, dance to a foolish beat in life. Now, it is a few ways to make good on this process to stopping the actions of youth foolishness.

I have learned that educating or schooling them to be the boss of themselves is the best way to go, not your way. It can be to your likeness if you see a youth that has the indications of wanting to be grown. It can trouble some parents/guardians and what can happen is the rejection of them growing up in a sublime way. You have fear of that happening to them possibly because of the mistakes you made, you do not want them to make. It is something some parents have to learn to step aside about.

Right now we are concerned more about them, and if it is displayed in a not so good way, what happens is conflict that may deepen the separation of communication between the two. To forewarn you: the wrong way to go is to try to act like you are their friend first, be the parent first. Then take it to the next level of them wanting to be your friend first then it is okay to follow suit. It is like my father use to say, "You will need me before I need you" and all the siblings I had knew that statement that was heard more than once.

Getting back to the point; it might be better to pay them to learn the things they can, that come out of the books I have written. You can join in to help and you may learn something yourself. That's right pay them as a chore to read and give you an essay at the completion. If they have any problems with understanding some things, let them know to let you know so you can help them work through it!

You can contact me if you find a mistake in a book, chalk it up as saying the author learns from you. Now, the pay for them can be something they like. An idea I have is to take them on a trip, to a concert, or to a show, or take them on an outing of their likeness and also. Maybe you would want to offer them a dollar amount that seems reasonable. By doing this you will be giving two or more presents of love all wrapped up in a gift that will be truly priceless. It will become even more priceless to them as they grow, thanks to the wisdom seeds planted in their minds and spirit.

Remember now is the time to offer the tools that may be needed. Do not be jealous of them getting more than you may have gotten in the wisdom state of growth.

Some would say that these books are a product of the "not to hit rock bottom in life process" to help people get to a level of having a kind of shield to protect them, for themselves first then protect them from others that may be somewhat out of control that want them to join in to become a part of the mess that can become a part of someone's life, that stops the blessings or cut them off from them.

With the help yourself (self-help) knowledge, you can keep yourself out of the way of getting in the trouble of spiraling down, rolling down, or monkeying around placement in life, so you cannot make the progress you were born to make. Sometimes reading the right kinds of books in life can help stop the sadness and the madness tour that some people go on that do not know better. The best part of this trip of growth is you can show up as you are and right where you are. You cannot beat that for a place to go to have a good adventure in learning.

Now is the time to understand it is not all about us all the time in life and what we've done. It is about what we look forward to seeing that others can do to pass life's magic wand or baton that does exist in an unseen reality. It is nice to know that you made sure they knew to be your own best friend before anyone else's, even before you.

The world was in much better shape before technology came along. The demons of the airways could not detour the election of the presidency or steal as much as they do from bank accounts using other folks' credit. This is just a thought to help keep us growing without some of the junk that takes us away from the natural things in life that we need to be sharing that are free.

If you are looking for a miracle it can just be a state of someone not going through a living hell. Some of the most unwise things people think is that they are waiting to get a blessing and ignore the fact they are so much more blessed than others. This is the unappreciative soul sin-drome that is a sin to have. It stops other blessings from taking place in their life. It is a part of the shame of it all, the trouble some people create for themselves that stops other blessings. That becomes a part of the sin nature when people get off tilted from knowing God's protection or spiritual skills.

One of the worst things people can have is an attractiveness to negativity. It can be looked at as the innocence of youth that falls into a trap because of them having a hard head and not being able to see or understand the consequences that will come behind their actions.

Get this completed, see your way out of this phase of work today. You can do it because God has your back. The Lord is giving people a break before they need a break. He can put you in charge of part of the government and the help they need to be repaired.

The government is in a very unhealthy state right now.

M-N
Be in the know

Your faith is the base to start your growth from and it helps to accept the changes in your life.

Step it up
To heal a mocking bird.

Who are the mocking birds? One of the Trumpees. In every presence or phase of dumbality you will find the void-noid, numb-dumb, lame-duck, plumb-dumb not including the some dumb butt, sin-drome. The spiritual wisdom b.k.a skills is the therapy that needs to be a practical treatment and rationalization of no self-deception. You can change, and once you do, you can be involved with ethical leadership. It comes with self-creativity and the readjustment of your reality.

Everyone gets broken of some pain;
What do you do with yours?

Sometimes, good natured people get pushed into the void-noid. It is a part of Satan's workshop. It works people over and may make them do things they wouldn't normally do, such as hurt someone. If they

164

don't know how to do what was invented by the greatest boxer of all times, called the rope-a-dope.

I think the complete meaning of it is you get somewhat roped in or put on the ropes. It is something they may not know you are there because you just got caught off guard. You may have fallen back being off balance. You need to catch your mind or bounce back, once you get your balance. At the same time the opponent gets worn out trying to hurt you. You learn from the mistake and come up with the winning move to stop their assault against you and get back in the winner's circle. It will be the dope on the rope because it can be a member of the void-noid, numb-dumb, lame-duck, sin-drome family.

It is the pain that harms people sometimes that helps them to turn hurt back on people. I have and was hurt. I had the broken heart problem of losing the one I loved. It happened more than once. The girl was, I thought, heaven sent for me and cupid put his arrows in her for someone else. It made me feel like a dope but I got off the rope.

This all happened before I got to the next level of school because when I got there, due to being passed over or up and out of that grade, they didn't want me to stay in the school any longer. I think it may have been because they had to get some kids out to make room for others. So whether they were learning or teachable or not they had to go.

My formal education stopped at the 4th grade. The dyslexia problem had a hold of me along with other attention deficit disorders. I was jacked up you might say. At home, there was the drama of an alcoholic father who also had a gambling problem. He also had some kind of army hang up that I guess came from the killing he did and saw that kind of kept him on edge at times, along with the lack of having an education. My mother had a limited education so it was a no help with the homework from school at home place to be at times. I was the second oldest of seven children but we did have love.

Where am I going with this? I kind of carried an anvil around my neck but at least it had a tattoo on it that told me that God loves me. It may have come by way of one of the old back woods country churches that I was in with my mother while in her womb, or after I was born going to as a little tike. I knew that I had seen the Lord in the way that he wanted me to see him and I know that anyone can see him especially when they are in pain. It may not stop the pain but it will comfort it to let you know when it is over the Lord will be there for you.

What must we do? We must believe in him then don't pay it forward to give someone else's your pain. The Lord keeps his for himself and he could have said, "Father stop this." I will let you think of what his father would have done.

I did get passed out of elementary school to the next level and was put in summer school. I remember the problem started at a movie where a worker in charge was showing what was an "R" rated movie because we had gotten tired of the ma and pa kettle thing. The school had a walk out about this and some of the people started some issues that got things a little uncomfortable. It was the 4th period walk out and a time of somewhat free for all fighting, if you had a beef with someone.

I had a beef with a guy because he didn't fight fair. I talked about it earlier in the book. He would fight people with brass knuckles, wrapped in a neck scarf, around his hand. I knew it and didn't think about fighting during what could be called a small scale riot. I wanted to hurt him; besides, he was somewhat of a bully.

Like I said, a friend stopped me but at the time the principal of the school caught me running down the hall and took me to his office. While he was looking out of the window at the confusion with his back turned to me, I took his swatting paddle and slipped it down my pants and got the hell out of there. As you know, it led me back to the placement of being locked up, though he was never able to hit anyone again with that paddle because I destroyed it.

Can I look at this as a break through that lots of people kind of look up to me for it? It means little to the readers but can you get inspired to do what you are in need to do to make changes. The principal seemed like he idealized the paddle to break the spirit of things people did and in the end lost it and it kind of broke his spirit.

Added to my learning disabilities was my bad report card grades. The best grades were Math and Handwriting. I think it helped mold my future because it gave me something to be proud of myself about and the proof of that shows, even though I am still a terrible speller.

M-N

Never ever play the "you can't get back your life" game. It is the dumb-dumb state you don't live in at all.

M-N

A mind will and can grow vital to the right things when you put the right things in it.

There is no doubt about the fact that there is a fight going on. It is a fight to keep yourself growing and going the right way in life and that is why you need help. We all need help at something but if we don't know or care we have problems. So in order to know for one's self that we can find what we need in the teaching in the bible that simply means **b**asic instruction **b**efore **l**eaving **e**arth that will tell you more than you will need to know and then some.

Excerpts from
The New Added Protection for the Development of Teens and Young Adults at Risk

Learn how to exchange the truth with others daily even if you find out you are wrong. Misery loves company. Tell them "I am allowing myself to share time with you. I am not here for the misery but for the healing and if misery tries to take over, I am gone far away."

This is a divine thing about life; when you look out for others in the right ways you are always able to look out for yourself better. It is better to be a helper than to be helpless.

There are awkward positions that we can conquer like knowing the difference between the needy and greedy; and helping the right ones that way you know who to look out for. Read between the lines of people and know who not to look out for.

This is a statement I would like to make known: people who act foolishly may not be a fool. However, by doing foolish things they do as fools do. They have to pay a price that sometimes sends them through hell. Warning: don't play with fire and you won't get burned.

Children must have the blanket of the Lord's shield over them. If they haven't received this, they may be wilding out of control. They must be placed in the Lord's net, as a lamb, with the right principles. If this is not done they follow worldly things and they get lost farther away from home and may not get back.

If someone can't be honest with self, why do you think they will be honest with you? It is foolish and it can complicate life.

It is time to pray for the bubble people that are trapped inside the wealth or security blanket they feel they have. God will deal with them if they aren't right. They are somewhat pitiful. In other words, forget about the people that have a need for greed.

Share the power of the rose; it is a symbol of love. Learn to fly like an eagle alongside a dove.

Free-dom; we have to learn how to celebrate the change of Christ Jesus, not just the birth of Christ; but the change and the way he had to do it. If he did what he did, you can do what you need to do.

I have written some small books with a big book bite that I hope you will read one day.

Work on yourself. Work through it to not harm anyone. To know change is there and everyone can do something good in life, even a towerist.

Looking into the future

The repercussions of the not good actions of things can be like a tsunami that is set in place that people have and need to be prepared for.

This book has a cousin being written about keeping the blood blue. It has been trying to get dressed to come to see people since 2004. Hopefully, we will be done in 2019. This book is enough to clear the air and get the stale stink out of it that makes anyone want to harm a child at any school, in Jesus' name.

M-N

Sometimes it is just as good when it comes from you when you tell yourself how proud of you, you are.

M-N

It is time to stop the melt down clown that Satan wants you to become. Say "I am not a clown or joker for the prince of darkness."

M-N

There is no magic in this book and it can't perform any miracles. It has the best understanding on the ways you can increase, and most of all keep, your self-respect. That is one thing you can live with and die with and keep forever.

Can this be one of the straws that broke the camel's back? It is like an action of a youth that is mimicking older people in a bad way who are killing people.

The latest present-day killings that are going on within families, as the break down takes place, have a "kill then stand up for what you have done" mentality as if it was done by someone other than self. I believe it was the dark shadow within that took control of the personal emotions and clouds their mind. It blindfolds them to not see their actions until it was over. This is the power Satan has over someone if they are not aware of it.

Being on top of the hill

There is one other thing that has a way of causing people to not feel complete. This is not knowing where you belong in life in the work and ministry the Lord wants for you.

The knowledge of being a hooded saint disciple will help you know that but if you add the *All Peoples Handbook* with it all of this wisdom even adds more love to the way you will do what you do.

You are now in or can grow to a phase of life where you can learn a lesson without anyone putting their hands on you to try you to teach you a lesson physically. You can teach a lesson without putting your hands on anyone else or doing any harm. This is the mature Godly principles in action that are evolving in you. Restoration has taken place and replaced some of the negative issues that you have possibly faced in the past, Amen!

We have to begin to revalue life because we have devalued life. It is not the right way to think at all.

#Enough is the Foundation

The book *#Enough is Enough* is the house that will be here soon! This book is enough to clear the air and get the steal sink out of it that make any one want to harm a child at any school, in Jesus name! Believe and receive this!!

What it's about

This book is also for anyone who feels like they have the tendency to harm anyone at all. No matter where it is at!

173

The main objective is the healthcare of the school, but you have the best reason on earth or not?!…

M-N

Let it be known, if you decide to latch onto on a new identity as a sky chief disciple you are now a part of the village that has the angels to rely on to watch over you.

This book may seem like one big chapter. However, it presents different levels of growth. This growth is to be used to spread the sunshine people are in need of!

I don't ever count me out, so you shouldn't either.

Fortitude!!

The inner fortitude came from the power to see through times of darkness and hardships so we all may sail on in life in our way, regardless to who we are and what we have. To know it will be alright one day is what we have to keep in mind all the time.

M-N

This is only one way of God's outward expression of love that he has for you to wrap his arms around you.

M-N

This book can really help anyone who has a blind need to harm anyone, even if they are a member of a group or an associate/in association of any kind.

A key that will help to move every mountain in your way is saying, "I am a new creation in Christ, I am a new being in Christ and Christ is a new being in me!"

It can happen

In life the parent is supposed to protect a child and the ugly part is when a parent isn't strong enough. It is a kind of painful shame. That is why you may need the added protection to help keep you safe or at least you become more equipped to survive and still remember you are not alone.

The nourishment will stick in your stomach, coat it and fill it!

M-N

There is no need to stay in the blind and dysfunction in life if you can learn your way around it! That is what wisdom is all about!

This book may be like sun screen that helps some people from getting burned. This process is also like getting a breath that you don't need to cross over to the other side, but you will not want to and thank God it got burned, so the walk way is gone!

This can be like a stop the traveler grid to not go certain places and do certain things!

Look at the fact if this knowledge help one person not commit themselves to becoming a killer, how wonderful that would be!

The Draw

What can be the biggest draw to this book? It is what it can possibly do to help, stop killing at school or even all over! If you have any kind of hang ups, let them go.

How many more killing in schools will take place in our nation? No more if we learn of this kind of justice that stop the injustice by the people who have coo-cooism that can make them want to commit this kind of crime urgent humanity. This is one of the better processes of anger management to get the control.

I had a mountain of information to give you and I still can if you like, but let this new gift the Lord has for the people of the world speak for Him!

This is the kind of news once learned that gets people hoped up! It gives the present of giving anyone open-mindedness to stop and revive their thinking so they will not have the wrong accountability to face.

This book starts over more than enough times because it really never ends. Now comes the time to stop the devil from causing the people to fall on their own scarce sword! It is a phase of a wealth of knowledge that may be somewhat cumbersome to read, but it is worth it!

There are parliamentary procedures to follow, but in extreme cases they too are meant to be broken! In the name of Jesus! Like it or not!

This did not come about from the fortitude of one man, but the Lord making available this wisdom and knowledge in this message to present it to all mankind.

This is faith practice: this knowledge creates the ability to grow to the level of living in the spirit and not in the flesh, Amen and Hallelujah!

Just a thought: now we are going to put Satan completely out of the picture. If he doesn't exist and let us look at ourselves as spiritual beings living in an earthly body, could this be one of the reasons why we find so much discomfort? Along with the discomfort comes all kinds of developmental processes of characteristics, miscalculations or misconceptions of certain parts of reality.

We need to be more concerned about in a sense the spiritual well-being our permanent existence then the physical well-being of our body in a sense, which is only an encapsulation of who we are. It is just a thought, if we take care of the physical body also, if we plan on being who we are forever or who we are going to be forever. We are going in an evolutionary stages of course, then we need to be more concerned in a sense about spiritual being.

I think this plan will help us in manifesting the growth needed to development and achievements of a good life also.

This message is a part of a new evolution that has involved/evolved in order to create a more peaceful atmosphere and give those who are lost on the highways and byways a chance to get back on a freedom train before it passes them by or leaves them in a place they cannot return from. So, get on board this is a part of a heavenly growth that needs to be accepted in Jesus name, Amen!

Do not miss this train, the freedom train may never come along again on this level.

If you are one who is feeling somewhat alone and a lot of discomfort about yourself within yourself, it is somewhat of a normal maladjusted growth development. Some go through it and have to readjust their own perspective about their inner being and their outer being so they will come together. At the same time you must realize it is only a temporary transformation of an unnatural state of existence that some of us go through.

Some may call it dating, coo-coo-cachoo stage that will sooner or later disappear in your life. It always happens and it may come back again, but you know how to deal with it now!

During this time you must always remember and never overthink the things that want to be present in your life that are negative.

There may be one other maladjustment of your functioning as a person with a normal level of misconception. It is having to deal with the "I want to be noticed blues" "I want to feel a better feeling within myself, about myself, and the way other feel about me that may be on the cuff of the turned inside out blues" that happens to people that causes them to create a rescission in themselves of some kind of depression, this too is a phase that people go through, though wanting to be noticed. When in all out actually and reality, you are noticed, you are always noticed, know the Lord notices you and that's the main one you want to be noticed by.

By the goodness in you, Satan wants to make you think that there is none, that people are not even aware of who you are and he wants you to be noticed, be noticed for doing something negative. He wants your attention more so then anyone or anything else.

The invisible culprit and demon of darkness wants you to put yourself in a position where you are being noticed as someone who harms someone and he is the one that you need to be aware of. He is the one that causes you to feel insecure and feel not good about yourself, so remember this is a temporary phase first of all, and you can eliminate that "want to be noticed" monster, Amen!

And also, it brings on that "I never want to be forgotten" phase of thought that is completely redundant to the facts of being ignorant. How can you be forgotten if you are labeled as part of the heavenly body, but in hell I guarantee you will be, be forgotten by everybody except by your predecessor, that predecessor named Satan.

We have more so wrapped everything up that I personally have thought about that I have experienced myself, now if there is anything that I left out and it is up to you to write it down and maybe make others aware another phase of negativity that we as humans are to deal with on a positive level and not on a negative level. So take and write out the rest of what I may have left out on a document and send it out to the world in a letter or a notification or even a book.

We must all remember that wealth is within and if it's developed without, on the outside basically that is a great thing too. Now, if we are barely getting by, barely making it, that's a fine thing too, so if you are a part of which I have lived with all of my life and more, being a part of that and any other thing poor-acracy, then don't let aristocracy bother you. There is nothing wrong with a life of poor-acracy if it is a life that is full of love, joy, and happiness, Amen.

Remember, poor-acracy is the opposite of aristocracy, whatever it is.

Don't be caught being somewhat of damn fool and harm someone who you really didn't have a need to. Get a copy of *How to Live with Less and Gain More*. Have a conversation with yourself today after you have read it and see how much wiser you can become.

Is it a strange thing that a black man came up with a possible solution for white youths that are harming each other at schools. Is it just the way the Lord works? He does not choose colors to bring forth His message, He just chooses people.

As you might say the solution to the problem of people killing other people does not just stop at the school killings, it refers to basically all killings.

Does it matter what race, creed, or color?

This process of creating a non-violent attitude towards students are not just limited to grade schools, high schools, but also colleges and any type of educational foundation.

Understanding all of things that have been presented to you in this book, helps you to deal with anything that come along with being dumb-founded and even having a panic attack. You are able to manage the panic in the emotions when you have an acceleration of negativity that is trying to divert you in an action of doing something wrong.

All of the things that have been combined once you develop your complete understanding of it and your self-analysis of it, gets you out of the stage of being dumb-founded so that one of the void-noid syndromes can affect you that send you down into a spiraling effect of negativity. We have achieved these things understanding the spiritual skills laws that the Lord supplies us with. That motivates us to not be as if we are some kind kamikaze that wants to crash and burn and harm others, in Jesus name. We are thankful for this wisdom and we share it with all people.

This present stage of growth on a spiritual level can do everything that needs to be done by depolarizing someone becoming or having bipolar symptoms or even if it is at a mature stage. It is that significant of instrument that develops harmony of understanding and the wisdom that is supplied by the Lord to overcome all of these attacks that negativity Satan brings upon someone even with those individuals who are close to you that may not know they are attacking you.

As I said before, you can be your biggest attacker when it comes down to trying to create some kind of way of defeating yourself unconsciously and maybe consciously. We can free ourselves from this kind of bondage by using these principles of spiritual skills learning tools and especially if we dedicate ourselves as a hooded saint disciple, a sky chief disciple, or become a disciple maker.

Well, we are coming to the beginning of our road and the end of creating the information so that you can create the solutions for yourself. You are determining the solutions that is needed to keep your life moving forward and developing everyone around you with a positive outlook on who you are and what you are about. Amazing that we can do so much as just humans, so we have to be thankful and then the fact of us having the spiritual creation in us, gives us more room to grow. One thing we must always remember we have room to grow. We never allow ourselves stifled in a situation that is no room to grow, with our every evolving and expanding and that is one of the main things we keep focus on and we can keep achieving.

Things have gotten to the point even in my life and I am talking about something personal, where anything that is said toward me to create a reaction of negativity, it doesn't work because it makes me a better person.

I utilize any of those approaching enemies in conversation that have a negative endowment that they want to place on me as I am supposed to inherent. I use that as a spring board to leap above and over as they are approaching me with something greater and better and this is one of the enjoyments of spiritual skills.

Spiritual skills it take you to a high where the earthly presence of negativity where people bring to you and expect you to earn up to it, it is not affecting you because you have been anointed and appointed another assignment that will not detour you that nothing can detour you from the work that you are doing in the body of Christ. It is a thrill and it is exciting.

Enjoy yourself and those that want to harm you or cause you not to enjoy yourself, you must not look at as not your enemy. They are their own enemy and they're in a fight with themselves that want to take you to a spiritual fight with yourself because of their fight. They cannot penetrate you with that because you are in a greater state of living in the spiritual realm of existence with the presence of the body of Christ and the Lord, Amen!

This is just like, not just the weathering the storm, but settling of the storm and taking the positive energy of the storm from it, that can come at you on a negative level. The excitement that is taking place is great, Love you.

This process of growth is like flushing all of the antibodies that come through a dimension of presence on a spiritual plains that is not of a Godly kind and given the negativity a taste of what you have as a force field to not allow it to penetrate within your living being.

You're dealing with things even when you get caught off balance to the point where the spiritual skills are kicking back out the negativity antibodies so that none of that unseen unnatural process will affect you in any way or any manner. That's what's happening!

This process is like the self-protection of the spiritual metabolism, we know that the physical metabolism will have its defects and one day it will not be ours anymore, it is only a temporary thing. Once we protect and learn to protect the spiritual metabolism of our being then we create a force only God needs to reckon with in the way He wants to. He teaches us how to let Him reckon with the spiritual force that we have within ourselves, so that nothing else can affect us even the prince of darkness that carries the powers of the negative force that, as I said before, can affect the physical being.

Now we are taking this to another frame of mind in existence in our reality that gives us more of one thing and one thing alone, that we live off, we need to survive and that is love growing. The magnetic power of love that comes from the heavens that we are attracted to and we are polarized to go toward in our daily lives.

This can be like ending a type of cancer that creates death within the spirit, not the physical, but the spirit. What we do is we protect the spiritual growth and do not let any kind of cancerous environment set up house so that it can tear down the house of the spirit that is within.

This is truly the blessings that are manifested through our faith and belief in the Lord that allows us to maintain the ability to increase the love factors on earth between each other no matter where you are from, nation, race, creed, color, religion or whatever. If you become a member of the body of Christ, these are the things you are endowed with to show others, Amen!

Some would say that there are three level in this writing, one reading it, two absorbing it, and three utilizing it and putting it into an active way of development. I feel this is part of the educational process that was developed through a phase of priesthood that entered into my subconscious being, that over rode that conscious level of thinking to be presented to you by way of the spirit that the Lord has placed in me to sustain life and growth in a multitude of developments. It can come out of this frame of work that will enhance of levels of love that can continue to grow and mature that has become stagnated due to certain elements or certain roadblocks. Now they are now being removed from the presence so that we can march even greater into a better future.

This is like presenting a strike three to Satan, he is out of the picture and a new day a new dawn is taken place and it needs to manifest throughout the world, not just from where you are or from where I am, but to where everyone can at least have an opportunity to be.

The development of this process of growth is determined by each and every one of us that it has been revealed to, to spread the news, the good news of the Gospel that the Lord has opened up another one of His floodgates to present us with another way to love ourselves and one another better, Hallelujah!

Can we consider this redevelopment of our spiritual DNA a technology or a level of increasing our spirituality? God has His way of creating His technology. Let's try to join them together and fuse them as the latest and greatest creations that the Lord is expressing to us to express ourselves that we have become endowed with from the creator.

In life, we can all be some dumb but not plumb dumb. Basically, we can have a division of being lost in a state of madness that has a development of craziness in it that is reflected out of us in given situations and in certain periods in time.

This too is a dilemma in which I had to face. Once I faced it, it became more or less prevalent in the development of it because I realized that if I continue to stay lost inside of myself, by me denying what's true about myself, I may never get out of the dilemma. It may even increase more of the process of losing the faculties of reality where it presents itself as crazy or completely dumb founded to the way of my abilities and not stop it myself from walking into foolishness.

Thank God for spiritual skills. They have a way of cleaning house inside of yourself of the mental deficiencies and dysfunctions that are there in some of us. It is just another thought I figured I would put out there just in case anyone needs it.

The last thing about the crazy stuff, somewhere in the middle. Have we gotten lost in the sauce or can we keep growing.

There is one other adjustment period that has to take place. As you grow sometimes you have to alienate part of the world away from you. At the same time, you have to maintain a visual of their understanding so that you will not make them feel as if you discarded them even though to a certain measure you may have somewhat. It's like dealing with someone who you know you have to cut off a path way to, to get to you and dealing with someone who you can allow to come approach you, but at the same time having a pathway that you have to let them know to go the other way in a proper manner.

This is what I call a step to it and step out of it process of dealing with people on an individual basis and this sometimes takes a little getting used to and a little adjustment. Sometimes you can become anxious on teaching someone who have processes of development of associations on different levels. They find themselves being offended by it when they should not and at the same time, those that should feel offended do not.

It is a growing process that I'm sure you may have a few trails and errors about. One day you will be able to master it, and when I say master it. I mean use the discernment you have within to know how to have the right response because you have the resources to apply them toward any given situation.

There is also another process and I'm not certain if you've heard of it, sometimes in order to love you have to run from love. Most people think you have to run to love, but there's a certain level of any process that requires to know how to hold it and know how to fold it.

Never fear the fact that you are running from love, if it is the earthly kind of love in order to receive a spiritual kind of love that is an endowment from the Lord. A lot times we will run to an earthly love and run from a spiritual love that the Lord wants to supply us with.

Now the reverse osmosis of this process when it comes to you, you will learn how to maintain the necessary level of when to hold them and when to fold them. It is beautiful thing when you start to develop it and it starts to enrich you from the inside out instead of wanting to be enriched from the outside in.

All of these things that you are learning is only another level of added protection that the Lord supplies us with as humans. No one has a different kind of perspective of it other than it is a blessing that we should share and if they do have another perspective about it, then there may really be aliens on this planet other than Satan, which is the number on alien. Maybe they are just influenced by it, well let's hope not.

In this quest to give the information that helps you to compromise on every level of what may enter your atmosphere from others. There are those who have the "I got to have the upper hand blues" or want to make it seem as if you either owe them something or they have more in a way to offer then you do. They have a way of wanting you to feel you are equal or less than they are, the "I want to have the upper hand blues" people are people who you have to learn how to, as hard as it may seem, bite your tongue or not bite your tongue, but bridle your tongue so that you won't let them know how they really are in order to save them some grief.

It is a kind-of a two-fold situation in communication to let someone know, I am not going to make myself feel a certain way. You want me to and I am not going to make you feel a certain way because maybe you want me to. Some people may want you to make them feel bad and so that they can have a reason to give an excuse to you that you were at fault or blame that is something that you were not. So, use the common sense that the Lord supplied and your mother and father wit so that it will go far beyond what others may be able to try to do to you in a way that they really may have done to themselves.

Another level of growth comes from when someone feels their level of maturity is the somewhat ultimate level of growth or the stage of "I know it all." To those who have made it to the level of a sky chief disciple or hooded saint disciple, it may be an immature stage.

The adjustment of even yourself recognizing these things and not being one to bash someone for it is a responsibility that you will have. There are different levels of growth and if they are not on your level doesn't mean you have the right to bash them or let them know that you are a long way from being an adult, especially when it comes down to someone accepting the fact that you are a child of God, which is very immature. Need I say more? No, I think you understand where I am coming from and thank you for understanding.

This is a ton of prevention that creates a multitude of growth and an enormous level of positive actions.

As a miner, sometimes you have to go down the same shaft to come out of a shaft to bring the gold to the surface.

If someone is in a spiritual war with themselves it has to be repaired. This came from no spiritual wisdom being applied to their life. We give them a kind of jump start to help by showing them a way to the intercessor bka Holy Spirit and it will put the light in place to move them out of darkness. It is like the home run that won the game in the Lord's name.

When it gets down to the re-tooling people are, in different ways, too cynical about changing. They may have fear of not knowing themselves or having to get to know someone who they did not want to have a relationship with in the first place. The faith building process comes in to take away the enemy that is fear that puts people in a self-incarcerated jail inside their head that is a war they have to fight. It spills out into life. So people have problems with others and that should not be a part of life. This is why the Lord puts spiritual skills together to give out keys to people to unlock themselves to know freedom.

We have to understand that we are now in the stage of delivery from an unseen plantation. This plantation is a place where a state of reality has been tainted and torn and infiltrated by the worse bully of them all. His name happens to be Satan. He bullies people on all levels. He has bullied people who are suppose to have responsibility and authority and is no respecter of persons as the Lord is. The Lord did not give any man that kind of authority. That is why we have to take our sights and look to another means of stopping the bullying, madness and sadness.

If we truly are our brothers' keepers then we look at them as a spiritual creation first and not what they have become in mankind's existence, whether they are butcher, baker, preacher, teacher, police, mayor or president.

We know that in some ways we all have been damaged and when we look at anyone, we need to first look at them as how damaged they are and you can't find that out until you know who the person is. In order for you to be able to clear the pathway you must look at yourself as your brothers' keepers then you look at the damage inside of you and what has damaged you. Then maybe there is a glimmer of hope that you can bring about a better understanding.

We have to realize that if we are at war with ourselves in one way or another, we have to learn to not project that on others. The spiritual warfare that goes on causes more of Satan's footprint and we have to eliminate as much of it as we possibly can. What I am saying is when you look at someone, look at them as a spiritual being who may be damaged more than you no matter who they are or what their authority may be. Then if you perceive them in that way it delivers you from being one who is pointing your fingers. You don't have to predetermine that they are your enemy and can never be your friend.

This will help you see how we misplace each other

Therefore, the controversy in the judgment and the laws that has been set forth before you and them are already in place. There is no opportunity for you to be able to come to a conclusion or agreement that you can be civil to each other. We can understand that if there is a situation we have to solve it in a meaningful existence and not let it escalate beyond recognition of having someone lose control and become demonized in a presence. What we do from there is stop the whole process as we approach ourselves consistently.

We are on this plantation of satanic behavior because that is what it is if you are not looking on a positive level or if you don't have any spiritual development which is skills, you have to look at it as yourself first and develop the loveoutayou first. So when you approach someone you can see the love in them no matter who they are or what they have done or how you feel because that is the way it is supposed to be.

Now we are getting off this plantation because the miracle has taken place and the miracle to spread this justice of the injustice starts with the miracle in you. There are some procedures and developmental processes that have to be gone through. We have to become educated and we need to become knowledgeable and aware of ourselves and then we can become aware of others.

If we are going through something, as I have been through, I would say dozens of traumatic experiences in my life before I could even present this I had to develop a way to present the loveoutame and the Lord has blessed me with that, even though I had to pay a hell of a cost.

I could help a multitude of people who are going through it if they understand and obey the rules and regulations that are governed by the Lord and mankind's laws you can always have in place without having to deal with them in an obnoxious way of making them your enemy and breaking them.

This is one of Satan's plans. He wants you to break mankind's laws so mankind can have a reason to intrude on your space and eliminate you from your space that is not supposed to be (or have you) incarcerated.

We can develop the steps to move forward and take down these walls that have been put up between us and the walls that tell us that we are locked on a plantation. We are now going to be planting the loveoutame seeds throughout our hearts and hopefully they will go or grow throughout the world one day.

The matador's cape has just been retired. For anyone who refuses to retire it, they may be retarded. What do I mean by the matador's cape? It is like the people who come out of their homes and the officers who come out to do their job have a confrontation and someone has the cape up already. The cape basically has the red sign of blood with a sword of some kind behind it to harm someone. This is them basically putting up a red flag saying, "I'm looking for a fight.

I'm looking forward to seeing if I can defeat or kill the bull in you."

Let's look at things in another perspective. If someone has trauma, or they have been through something, they are automatically lifted up where their feet are not planted on the ground. What takes place then is the balloon fills with helium and raises them up. This is because of a trauma. The more trauma that they are unable to resist they get another balloon lifting them up higher. This is anyone at any time that could be facing this. At the same time, they are trying to figure the problem out and come back down to earth but they are unable to.

Negativity is all about taking someone off balance, putting the fear in them, not giving them an opportunity to get their balance. They are afraid of their own self-destruction or someone else destroying them. They become apprehensive and repulsive and defensive to others. What do we do to help end this? We have to realize that there may be a curse from their forefathers. They may have an insecurity or a misguided compass in life where they don't really understand what they are doing or where they need to be.

We hope to give people insight but first look at them as someone who was or could have been lost before they understood how to become a spiritual being, someone who has a presence of being able to find a way to resolve issues. We have to look at them as our brothers' and we are their keepers.

Instead of coming out with a cape when we walk out of the house we come out with a cupid bow and arrow. As we see someone or are confronted with someone who we feel will cause negativity to take place we automatically are shooting out our arrows into the balloons and release the helium so they can come back down to earth so they can be planted firmly on ground. They will know that both them and you are harmless.

This is how God's therapy works

What has developed is the loveoutame cupid syndrome that has taken place to head off, stop and defeat the negative process of coming into a situation. If we all think about the loveoutame cupid syndrome before re we leave home each morning or even at home between family members, we may find ourselves living in a better world than we ever thought we could live in, rather than living with a red indication as if we want war or we want to fight the bull or we intend to get the bull out of you.

We have been approaching things in the wrong way for centuries. This has become a part of Satan's plan for us to continue living this way. This is why we are losing so many people in the dieconomie process.

Venture not out of your space until you have understood that you have cupid's bow and arrows to deflate the helium. Once you have understood these facts, look up and see how many balloons filled with helium have been lifted above your head and taken your feet off the ground and you can start shooting them down.

To use the kind of metaphor to help end a level of spiritual war is good therapy and all it takes is a vivid imagination.

The bottom line with the work I do is, the Lord equipped me after I became a willing vessel. You are really the ones who had me hired to do this because it was something that needed to be done. We needed someone who could put it in a format that all could understand.

I am a crisis intervention specialist but you are really the one who has to denounce the principles that Satan has put upon your life. I am thankful to you if you work with me or hire me. I am also thankful to the Lord for allowing me to be the vessel he uses to guide you through an era of ungodliness and negativity to reassess and redevelop a cultural status to overcome anything that comes to us by way of one of Satan's storms.

I am thankful for the opportunity and then you show me the loveoutayou. I can't ask for anything more than maybe a pittance to help me survive through the trying times.

I hope it is something that you feel good about: the fact that this is really your idea in the first place. Throughout generations we have developed prayers. Your idea is to get answers to prayers and these are the answers that you have been given by the blessings of the Lord. You have prayed for someone to bring an answer as they prayed for Jesus, the Messiah, the King to relieve pressure, torment, trouble and hellish situations on earth.

The Lord has made mini me's. A mini me is basically someone who has been given the Lord's foresight because of prayers, to be able to give relief to the body of Christ and increase justice for all in many different ways. As I would say, I am just a branch off of the tree. There are other branches coming off of me and I thank God for them.

Could we say this is your loveoutame that is taking place because of your prayers and the writing that I do? I think we can. I also think we can be safe in our sound decision-making.

There is nothing like a sound state of mind and a heart filled with joy and a spirit that soars like you are still a little boy or girl. There is nothing in the world to compare to those feelings when you share them with others and you have a true idea of who you are.

Now that you have become educated you can become an educator. No longer are you polarized or stigmatized or drowning in the victim's level of not knowing. You are able to speak boldly with the principles that guide you to a stronger person that you have always been.

As we say, we lose a little something out here because Satan is like cryptonite. We are super people in our own ways. We have come through the evolution of becoming more humane daily. We never want to lose that. We want to keep moving forward. In other words, the spiritual skills kill cryptonite as on placement in a sense of sins and Satan.

Now we develop our own new and better concepts as we move forward into a new millennium, especially being the individuals who are receiving the change of the world's perspective and has a responsibility of putting it back into a place where it needs to be. Become not just learned, become a teacher and a sponsor to yourself so you can show someone else how to do what you do as the Lord would do.

A wake up call

Every time you pick up a gun or riffle or any kind of weapon of steel to use it for, think of it as if it got melted down to become a branding iron that is hot. If you think you are going to do something wrong. Think of how it may feel if it was put on our body and left a mark saying "you are in hell."

This book provides information on the presence and stages of a dieconnomie that was created by Satan. It is a place that overrides the actions of some people to cause them to kill others. It can be stopped with the wisdom in this book and the book, _The Biggest Collar_.

This is one of the reasons why the three levels of discipleship are offered, to increase your personal defense skills against the attacks that Satan has for all people. They will give you a hand up out of darkness that is a pathway to misery and pain with death as the end goal. So say hello to one or more being the Father, Son or Holy Spirit (b.k.a. the Comforter). They can show up after you in any one of the books at any time that may be a right time.

Heads up

Condemnation of self must stop. So many people condemn others. Don't let anyone do this by you paying it forward in your life. Some will hear and do; some will hear and not do. Which one will you be?

Work History

There came a time after I became a father I had to help support my family. I took on all kinds of odd jobs such as in the summer I worked on a small farm. It was a job. I kind of made friends with the people I worked for. This was after I was free from wanting to be a headache to myself and others. I worked for the people for a while then I found out what the guy who hired me did for a living. He was a retired police chief of Solon, Ohio. I was also working for his son-in-law who was at the time the mayor of the same city.

I didn't know any of this at first, because all I knew about them was they were some of the nicest people I had ever met and they showed me friendship. They were fun to work with and paid me as I felt was a good dollar for my labor. I came back to help out for a few more years. I still get in touch with the son or grandson sometimes. I still have a good relationship with them.

The great thing about the good old days is you could ask people if they had any work and if they did they would give you a chance.

You are in contact with the best immigration lawyer there is to kick out Satan.

It is time for some people who may be lost in a dimension of ungodly growth to stop hoolah hooping and get out of that ring of what can eventually turn into fire. No one needs to jump through rings of fire doing the hoolah hoop.

Unlock yourself from that phase of existence if you are there. No one needs to be a copycat about anything that is ungodly and creates harm, pain and death for others.

These are the blueprints that have come from the architecture of life that wants life to continue forever and ever. Read now to receive a purpose of your plan of development of your life.

These are the keys to human rights and the first right is everyone deserves to live a full, blessed and happy life.

If we lead by example and show the rest of the world how much more we have developed a culture of love then the rest of the world will want to do the same. So let's bring about a new example of decreasing killing in our country.

A forget me not

Do some kind of exercise to keep your tension live at a place that is forever manageable. By the time you complete this book there should not be any twists and turns that try to get you to harm anyone.

The blind can see once you begin to understand this eye opener that the Lord gives and no one else including Satan can take it away. It can be placed in the 3rd or 4th place of love: 1. Agape; 2. Eros; 3. Philia; and 4. loveoutame. I am thankful to my Lord that he has fulfilled the cries and helped dry up a part of the tears in my eyes.

This is one of God's cease fire peace treaties to have with yourself regarding all others, no matter who or what it is about. The death angel or the grim reaper doesn't matter when this treaty is called upon in the heart of anyone with the loveoutame flower. It creates a heavenly power that gives the control of one's self over to the angels in heaven to take charge of the life matters and stop the death matters concept of Satan.

S-N

The Lord is friending you. Are you willing to accept him? This is only another way he shows his love.

To the misguided at heart: get back on track

There are so many mis-developed friendships that start with someone abusing themselves in a way of not knowing the power of knowing no. That is right now because some people's biggest enemy becomes self. They do not want to believe in "no." People must know that it is Satan working and learn to love the word "no."

There is a fact that it is so understated in a way. It made some of leaders of our nation inspire me to write a book titled, _The Power of Knowing No._ It teaches people how to say no and to know themselves. If more men said no to and stop trying to make someone accept their advancement, there would be lots less harm to more people.

Cause me to write about this.

You could say one of the greatest battles some people may ever get involved with is the battle when you want to learn whether there is love for you between someone else and yourself. You find out that there is a battle between you and yourself. You put the other person in between that and they have no way of responding properly. You get angry at them because you are not able to get an answer from them that you want. Actually, you need to be getting an answer from yourself first place. It is no and that is unacceptable and someone seems to get lost out of reality. They feel that you are owed something by someone else.

You are really owed something by yourself and when they want to leave you in that battle alone. You turn around your understanding and get angry at them and want to harm them because they want to exit stage right. You want them to not exit and stay in the fight and it's not their fight in the first place. It raises hell to a degree where it causes devastation and abuse. It may get violent and maybe the next thing you know it is a ball of confusion that you can't get out of because of what is more than a spiritual war. You may have a schism that adds to the problem that you had in the first place. Of course it is the opposite then you have a double indemnity of damnation in the non relations, whether it ended or never was in the first place.

Remember to learn how to not have battles with yourself in the first place. Say no before you get involved. Then you will not have to get involved with a battle with someone else. In other words, don't fight for nothing when there's nothing really worth fighting for. Leave things alone and people alone. Get the love you need for yourself before you try to include anyone else in your life.

Muse news

Nothing I do is worth the paper it is written on unless it is shared with someone who can learn from it.

Muse news

As time goes on Satan keeps retooling. This is a part of the Lord's retooling program because he will always stay steps ahead of Satan.

Muse news

It is neither here nor there but at the same time was having closer to the earth than ever before or afterwards when the Lord took the tower down.

Muse news

The books I write are not for entertainment purposes. They are to help people improve their life to get it on a more happy, healthy and secure place in the spiritual realm of things. This will allow the state of life to become more wholesome.

Muse news can become very useful

To make it plain and simple, the government gives tax breaks or so they say but they only go so far.

Moving on to a new kind of momentum

Know that nowhere else can you get these kinds of breaks I am talking about. After you join the Lord's dream team the Father, Son and Holy Ghost there are a lots of deductions. No worrying or depression; you do not have to lie. You do not have to steal. You do not have to kill. You do not have to be foolish. You do not have to be crazy. You do not have to be lazy and the list goes on and on. So who has the best deductions when you compare mankind's to what the Lord has to offer?

Muse news

Know that our differences can be our strengths.

Muse news

Time is a friend to all things good and what a friend to have in writing. It gets better every day.

Muse-News

Rest on the edification of this scroll.

Muse news

Know that giving makes a lot of people happy. Try it; do not judge.

You know that new words that begin with "schism" can cause you to become a snap fool to increase sickness, flat-out or right out to the road to sinning.

Are the books something the Lord wants you to have?

Why do people kill? They are out of control. This can come from something bad that happened in someone's life that is a part of trauma. It can sicken people to make them hate and/or act full of foolishness, temporary insanity, or being somewhat crazy. They may act like a predator or a terror.

The pain some people have the devil makes use of if we do not stop it. It is at least self-predicted or predictable. It all does not matter if people had to fix all of this kind of stuff in their life. God gives the power to stop the madness to get control. You can be all that others are and then some in a good way.

If you are in control you won't kill. Let yourself be used by the power of the Lord to protect you from doing wrong things. Then everyone can know how much love you are capable of showing to help keep you going in the right direction in life.

Keep it real

People can stop using their ignorance as an excuse to be a fool and be proud of it at the same time. That is what happens after some people have done the wrong thing. They want to own up to it to so-called protect themselves from whatever may come their way next. It is a part of the old blindness that keeps out of sight to steal the daylight from so many people. It disappears and never returns again to the lives of the innocent to harm them can be stopped.

What is the best tool? Faith, belief and the imagination to work on fixing inner torment to the level of using spiritual skills. It becomes a wrap to not exist in the emotions of one's self and it remains harmless. It is a place that puts begins after the discovery of who you really are, with the news that has come upon your life.

It is better to know of the Lord's next stop when he returns back to earth. You can also wait there at a place in the heart.

This is the process of returning home if you have been lost outside of yourself or inside of yourself. It means to be home on or in a place called Zion. It is a place inside of your heart that you can find a haven of rest, peace and love to go there as if you were a lost sheep who has found their way home. It is heaven's gift to refresh you.

If this news is coming from one of the greatest locations in the nation to show the world who does not know where the greatest location in the world is. It is inside of their heart. Then the loveoutayou has always been there. There are so few who know or there are so many more who need to know.

Foresight to become complete

As the wise men traveled together they shared the knowledge of the world. This is why the book shares some of the same knowledge to make it better for everyone. In *The Biggest Collar* you will find some of the information to help people grow healthier in life. All you have to do is look for the two wise signs. It is only a few chapters in the back of the book but it may put a new light on the light you can see already in this book.

Each book is named after the three wise men: 1 Caspar. He was the king of India and it goes with *The Biggest Collar*. 2 Melchior. He was the king of Persia and it goes with *#Enough*. 3 Balthasar. He was the king of Arabia and it goes with *Help to Stop Bullies' Bullets*.

To All

Whether you do or don't go into a house of God you can get something good out of this knowledge.

So if people do not want to be in fellowship it might be that they have not so good self-leadership skills. If you want to get a quick fix for this process learn to follow the Lord, he is the real leader. Read more about this. Jeremiah 17:9 can give you some information on that. Know that at the end of life the value of life is determined by how much of it was given away. How much are you giving away? Are you giving away enough?

A good set of starter tools can be found at Galatians 5: 6. Yet another place you can read up on this information is John 13:35. A platinum rule is a peace offering for towers to even get the lost sheep in Towers out of the devil's lair. To be so saved saved by the Lord but at the same time leading people to suffer has a price to be paid. If it is a kind of gateway to the falling into Satan's trap for others that may lead to hell. For them the blame will not be the same like the thief on the cross.

I have set up the level of knowledge

in this book to reflect three in one book.

To anyone who would like to know what all my writing is about. It is about defeating and helping to stop the injustice on all levels to help people stop being used by Satan. You can be used by Satan in all kinds of ways some of which you may know, some you may not. It is only the shepherd in me that causes me to do as my Father in heaven would do (Isaiah 53:2-6).

There were other wise men that visited Jesus after he got to be an adult. Was one of them connected to my spiritual DNA? To be honest I think we all are if we are believers. Why did they go to Jesus? it was probably to create for clarity in the direction of their gift with a better understanding about it and its use.

I tried to write this book as a very well developed opera so people can sit back and enjoy it and be able to relate to how it may help their life through enlightenment. I will testify that I believe I could be one connected to the spiritual realm that adds to what I am doing. I hope it helps you also.

I am not a perfect human but this level of life helps stop lots of drama and negativity, so it does not affect my spirit and heart. That gives me stability on a healthy and wise growth pattern.

It seems as if I was walking in someone else's shoes when I first started the reread to this book. At the same time it seems as if I hadn't read this book life would have been a little more terrifying in some ways.

After reading this book, we are now ready to imagine that we are in a new era of a birth canal, a spiritual birth canal as a child that will come out. As a child of Christ as we enter into the world the only thing that we need to cry about is the light that shines so brightly that it harms the child. It may not be the fear that harms the child because of being born in sin that causes them to cry.

Now we are being reborn in a spiritual nature where spiritual reality and the light is the thing that affects us in a good way. It is the Lord's light that we see once we come out of a dark pathway. So if we cry it is a good thing not a bad thing.

We claim victory over the healing power that we receive. We come out with our arms open to the world and the love that it has for us. The love that we are going to return to will cause us to claim victory over spiritual illnesses. We claim victory over mental illnesses. God knows if you have a physical illness you may find possible cure but definite victory over that also, in Jesus' name. This is our new present day stance that we take as children of God.

They say that love is better the second time around. Could this be guarantee with God only? Sometimes the earthly love we find with each other can be sweet and sometimes bitter. The Lord's love is always enduring with the sweetness of the fragrance out of a flower. It is the loveoutame flower that blossoms and grows throughout anyone's life who is ready to accept it. This flower that the Lord offers us should be accepted by all so we can plant flowers in a Garden of Eden one day ourselves that he will allow us to go in without being harmed by the Cherubims. Hallelujah.

To cover every base that you can in protecting yourself, make sure that you get a check up on an annual basis for your health care. Something as you might think as insignificant as having low blood sugar can increase your anxiety. It can increase your tenseness and cause you to evolve into some kind of radical individual. It affects your nervous system to a certain degree to protect you from any possible kind of negative feelings of emotions that have become a place in your physical being. It can possibly even affect you to a degree where it is tough teaching in a negative spiritual realm. Keep your blood sugar at a normal level thank you.

Let's get our glucose levels in balance. When those levels are not balanced it depletes energy and causes people to lose self-control. It is a serious issue that we must confront and accomplish so that we will not be addicted to this placement of having an odd system in place.

Thank you for caring about yourself because when you care about yourself you care about others. If you can't care about yourself in certain ways you won't care about others. These two negative things may be bound and tied together in ways that cannot be explained but they do exist.

This is a part of the resurrection of life.

The bullet bully sin-drome is a state of being on a Satanic presence of action. It can affect anyone at any time it gets the opportunity to catch someone at a weak state of existence. They are not aware or in control of themselves. The darkness and the power that it possesses overruns the individual who does not have enough light to be able to shine. Their presence of action can be caught up in the unnatural mannerism of harming someone. That is what this is all about, stopping the presence of the darkness over the unknown presents light that is stuck inside of someone. It needs to come out so they would be aware to avoid negativity and obtain and maintain self-control.

Do not be a ding dong because the itch is dead, the itchy witchy finger to pull a trigger itch is dead. Long live the victory of the human race to keep denying a Satanic itch. The itch comes by way of someone who has been taken over by a dead spirit of a warlock or witch. (repeat this three times like a song)

This will give you a possible experience in living that you have been looking for. Without the right information your judgment will be cloudy. This gives you a way of un-clouding your judgment, and gives you an experience for living.

Know that the ceiling and visibility are unlimited. This came from Uncle Bush and it has stood for eons and will stand for eons.

M-N

This is from one bush to another bush to help carry out the wishes of the first bush born between both of us. We hope this develops a kinder and gentler world, from the wisdom that has been placed in writing in this book.

It is nice to know, even if you never met someone they have become a part of your life in a big way. It makes you feel good that there are so many people that you may never know who are alive and have lived.

We're all a big part of a greater plan in preservation for man. It is beginning to look like everyone can contribute a component of love, of presence, of knowledge, of wisdom, of truth and of freedom.

We all can rebound back even after we have made a mistake and we came down for whatever reason there may be. So let's give it another chance to become better humans even when we make mistakes, or give ourselves another chance at the truth in it all.

I have made enough mistakes for myself, God knows I have. If I didn't feel he wanted me to give myself another chance, I may have not been here to present what is being unveiled and what is being lifted to give to the Lord as a present within the writing that you are reading.

I can't wait to see what others can do once they find their freedom to do this, even though they may have been in some type of bondage. That doesn't matter anymore because you are free now. Give God his credit while you are on earth and receive his reward when you go to heaven.

New News

The Lord can make a mule talk. This is a part of how to make a person wiser than a mule with enough wisdom to choke a mule. If the Lord can make this happen, can mankind get understanding from it to make one wise if they got a belly full of it.

One of the best parts of this teaching may be the fact that you can catch up with your life again if it has gotten away from you. I testify to the fact that I am thankful to the Lord for helping me get it back before it got lost forever.

A good way to know to go

Now when you close one book you open up another that the Lord had made for you to be a part of your life. The book that gives all written knowledge of what you've done. You do not want to be known as an individual who has taken someone else's life. It may have been a life that the Lord had plans for in a mighty way to do mighty things. That means you have set back his promise but it will get done.

Satan wants to try to eliminate as many things as possible that the Lord can get done. There is a such thing as long-suffering. This long-suffering is when he wants someone to wake up from whatever negative reality they are in. It would only last for a night as he said in and with the crying of the tears in weeping.

When someone does something wrong and they don't repent for it they create a long-suffering situation for themselves and or not forgiving someone they may create a long-suffering for themselves. It is a kind of way of punishing someone in a frame of existence before they have a permanent punishment on their lives.

Remember God doesn't need you to do his work for him on a level of harming someone in need of help. He wants us to know the sickness of others to be able to stop ourselves from taking someone's life. Satan wants a different outcome to create an episode that can ruin your epitaph of what you are going to be in the future. You don't need this on your resume, "I was a murderer for no good reason." Eliminate that chapter in your life you know.

What can I say about this method? I have faith that it will help to deter some people from wanting to commit crime because of a new presence of love. This is the will of the Lord to be a part of something he has put in place to stop sin that leads to crime or crime that leads to sin.

M-N

Say to yourself from time to time, "May the end game of Baal be damned. I will not worship it.

M-N

Laughter is the healing power for corrosive elements in life. Human is the head that shake off any bad tail!

This is added to the end of 4 books so that you will know to further your education and teaching. It is time to lay hands on the 20/20. after that one it is ending the world's deadliest sin when it appears in 2019.

To know good news and have patience to use

The main curse of humanity is the poverty of not knowing your spiritual wealth that is not dead. It is worth more than all the material wealth on Earth. If you do not have a presence of understanding about that you are poor and it is the true crime in life. There is no bigger one than to be at a place that has no love that can last forever in one's life. It is really the biggest and only poverty in life no one needs to have and that is why that is what has been happening to people all over the world. So can we change it the face of this problem for the Earth. If you help the Lord make thank you personally I believe can you?

Today here is the opportunity that comes out of or a miracle of understanding

It is my hope that everyone and then some who reads this will have the wisdom to glorify the Lord's word in the flesh to make themselves able to poke holes through the darkness until the light comes through!

News to be used

This may be the Lord's gift but he wants you to unwrap it for him and share in the good of it. In his son Jesus' name, please participate and all are welcome!

The 2020 book is the, or an, eye opener. If we pray to know that what mankind has done it can be forgiven by the Lord then the rest is up to us to see how much good can come out of the work we do to help ourselves and the future generations of the world.

News to be used!

The greatest part of all of this is we are developing a collective forgiveness plan to bring the human race up to a better level of loving one another.

Muse news

The doves of the Lord are released in these books

Explanation has been given.

The 20/20 recovery of the world in preparation of the Lord coming back!

What can be one of the best things learned it is to own up to our responsibilities no matter how small or large and or but to also never leave out love.

New News Center

Now it is time to know when you do not have to mean harm to be harming people so think about what you may not need to do and do not do it.

The four books are in agreement they are somewhat as one that can be known as The Four Seasons mixed on whatever level that comes to one's mind it is your choice: winter, spring, summer or fall. The presence of "I can weather the weather, whatever the weather." In order to help put a stop to all kinds of 1. massive killing, 2. single killing, 3. two dual killing, 4. self killing. Time is not out time is in for living a full life, as was meant to be for everyone the Devil is a Lie to be one of the Lost with adding to his the economy. His lie has exposed.

The books I have written are like team players. Every time you read another one, you add more of you as a member to the body of Christ.

Muse news times 2

That what can't kill you can make you stronger if you face up to it and follow the fact that one day you will find your talent and use it so do not fear the next opportunity that will come your way.

Muse news

Remember that in the darkest moments humor is open to your connecting with it. It can be the greatest fun.

Whatever tries to choke you out of life or someone else with the noose around your throat, forget about it. It may be a big pill to swallow but you can. It is not about you it is about a "we thing," because you are not alone. It will take all hands on deck to make some of the things right in this world. All of us may have been tricked or tripped up by a kind of fire and brimstone that harmed us. I am sure in the past I have had hell misery put on me.

It was my cross to bear, no matter how big or little. I had to face up to and bounce back and bear the weight. However, the Lord did help me carry it.

We will take the complete dead spirit of all creation and add them up to give a level of how bad the problem of we put out is along with what we have been getting back in America.

Now if you have the presence of being a part of the Godly we movement. This is one of the wise men book titles with the name of Melchior. It is a preference to the gift for the Lord. That is what it can be to you!

To show up on deck you will need to see a new horizon of schooling. This can be found in the other two books and the book that has a title called The 20/20 vision for the peoples in America's future to be released in 2019. You can email me if you're interested at Bound To Heaven publishing Ministries to get a copy.

Muse news

I will say the wounded make the best soldiers. They have been there and learned to stay out of the way of our enemy and can also teach others. That is why Satan wants to take them out.

To complete this book you may want to read, _The World's Deadliest Sin: Towerism_. After you complete that one it is recommended that you read the book about America's Comeback 2020.

The first three books had to be stopped to let people catch a moment in time, before things got new once again.

Remember to never let lift stop on you because we can never get enough.

I know I can make a mountain out of a molehill as you can when we are in the will of the Lord.

I wound like to introduce you to the Annex of all other four books

It is a book titled:

Ending the World's Deadliest Sin: Towerism
(Starting in the USA then the world)

The four books that this book need to be attached to are: *Help to Stop Bullies' Bullets*, *#Enough*, *The Biggest Collar* and *The Comeback of America 2020*. These books have a part two that completes the four. I put this in a context like that because it is the last of the knowledge that goes with all of the books. To some people, it can stand by itself. We can say it is like a chess game with this as the last move.

As an example, if you know about the game of chess, and you look at a picture that was painted in 1800s, you see the king has the last move to win the game. It was a novice's turn to move but the other player was a professional. All you could say is it was a great looking picture. This is the same way with life. The king has the last move to check mate and win. So if we know what is good for us we move with him. To see the picture for yourself look up 'one more move chess' on the web to see a picture that is put together to inspire everyone.

Is this another way to look up to the truth we can trust? Now reattach this book to the back of the other ones. Is this also the message to help us detach ourselves from the things that could kill us or others? Keep living for the next move of the king. Life is on and not to be turned of. It is a good time to come out of all darkness. Now it is your move.

Again, reattach this fifth book to the four that add to the grace and truth. See yourself detach from the death of the bones of the collarism or just wanting to be of a human kind of development. And not a spiritual development of a presence in a human existence.

This book has been made of less than one half of the other parts of the four books it goes with. However, it is all for one and one for all.

These are my seeds I am planting for showing up for Christ. If you find some good seeds here, do not look over them, share them.

M-N

We had a process of suffering in life that some want to become normal from. They first need to be healed in a way to stop whatever is wrong, without hesitation.

This is for the good, bad and the ugly, it doesn't matter, to end the war within. If you have ever experienced it, the prayers are open to receive you.

To see; to know; to show; to love

I like to think that I can stay in the right flying state of mind as if I am practicing an angel dance without falling out of control. If I don't feel good about my conscious and emotional level at times I can spin myself and wish the cares of what maybe troubles away. I can do this over and over again as I go around and around. It frees me from the harm that wants to consume me with negativity. So I encompass myself and become a big spinning top myself. If I get tired of spinning myself around before the unhealthiness stops, and/or until it does, I can use my little spinning top which is also a therapy toy.

To help myself, at the same time, if I have a negative state of thought to go with the emotional and physical side using the release of the mental side of a self-healing therapy to help stop pressure from going through my halo, it can free me from what I do not want to think about that is wrong.

You can sit back and use your imagination to see yourself spinning around and around. You will know you are free from a sin debt that Satan wants you to incur.

The thought of the process of negativity going up through the halo outside of my thoughts and dissipating and disappearing forever is what will be considered a release valve to get the pressure out. It is a God given therapy that man is allowed to use with faith to guide all people to a pathway of righteousness.

At the same time, I am getting my healing with my spiritual skills, my mental and physical with this kind of food. I am taking care of my mind and soul by releasing the cupid in me and the Godly part of the arrows to target all so I can share the loveoutame, as I go about my life to show how I can feel good about myself and others around me!

This is God's way of helping all people get a full recovery of the wounds of pain and hurt on all levels in life peoples are exposed to. It even helps the towerists slide down out of the towers, big ones or little ones. Now the way out is made to stop the fear of harming one's pride as they slide down or come down and grow up instead of trying to fake it as if they have some kind of power and guardianship over others, along with being released from Satan's toehold and the noose, if it got that far.

To help anyone understand more about the prolific surrounding this therapy you can find all the additional details in the book, _Ending The World's Deadliest Sin: Towerism_.

> Does mankind still refuse to
> become aware of this truth?

Act I:4-8
4. And being assembled together with them, He commanded them not to depart from Jerusalem, but

to wait for the Promise of the Father, "which," He said, "you have heard from Me;
5. "for John truly baptized with water, but you shall be baptized with the Holy Spirit not many days from now."
6. Therefore, when they asked Him, saying, "Lord, will You at this time restore the kingdom to Israel?"
7. And He said to them, "It is not for you to know times or seasons which the Father has put in His own authority.
8. "But you shall receive power when the Holy Spirit has come upon you; and you shall be witnesses to Me in Jerusalem, and in all Judea and Samaria, and to the end of the earth."

There are books I have written that helped to lead people to the promised land of knowing they are loved by other people and the Lord.

To get more books to help you stay in the right lane of life go to boundtoheaven.org.

Acts 20:24 – But none of these things move me; nor do I count my life dear to myself, so that I may finish my race with joy, and the ministry which I received from the Lord Jesus, to testify to the gospel of the grace of God.

Philippians 4:17 – Not that I seek the gift, but I seek the fruit that abounds to your account.

9 781793 252081